50 Vegetarian Salads Recipes for Home

By: Kelly Johnson

Table of Contents

- Greek Salad
- Caprese Salad
- Quinoa Salad with Roasted Vegetables
- Chickpea Salad
- Beet and Goat Cheese Salad
- Waldorf Salad
- Mediterranean Orzo Salad
- Thai Papaya Salad (Som Tum)
- Caesar Salad with Homemade Dressing
- Spinach and Strawberry Salad
- Mexican Street Corn Salad (Esquites)
- Kale Salad with Lemon Tahini Dressing
- Watermelon Feta Salad
- Lentil Salad with Roasted Vegetables
- Tabouli Salad
- Asian Slaw
- Avocado and Tomato Salad
- Roasted Cauliflower Salad
- Pasta Salad with Pesto
- Moroccan Carrot Salad
- Potato Salad with Dill Dressing
- Cucumber Salad with Yogurt Dressing
- Broccoli Salad with Cranberries and Sunflower Seeds
- Edamame Salad
- Mango Avocado Salad
- Radicchio and Orange Salad
- Spinach and Artichoke Salad
- Israeli Salad
- Brussels Sprouts Salad with Maple Dijon Dressing
- Roasted Eggplant Salad
- Black Bean and Corn Salad
- Tabbouleh Salad
- Spinach Salad with Strawberries and Walnuts
- Fennel and Orange Salad
- Thai Noodle Salad

- Roasted Vegetable Salad
- Grilled Peach Salad
- Quinoa Greek Salad
- Cauliflower Salad with Lemon Tahini Dressing
- Tomato Basil Mozzarella Salad
- Asian Cabbage Salad
- Pear and Walnut Salad
- Spinach and Quinoa Salad
- Citrus Avocado Salad
- Kale Caesar Salad
- Roasted Beet and Goat Cheese Salad
- Chickpea and Avocado Salad
- Mexican Corn Salad
- Herbed Potato Salad
- Cranberry Almond Quinoa Salad

Greek Salad

Ingredients:

- 4 medium ripe tomatoes, cut into wedges
- 1 cucumber, sliced (peeled if desired)
- 1/2 red onion, thinly sliced
- 1 green bell pepper, seeded and sliced
- 1/2 cup Kalamata olives, pitted
- 1/2 cup feta cheese, crumbled
- 1/4 cup extra virgin olive oil
- 2 tablespoons red wine vinegar
- 1 teaspoon dried oregano
- Salt and freshly ground black pepper, to taste
- Fresh parsley or basil leaves, chopped (optional, for garnish)

Instructions:

1. **Prepare the Vegetables:**
     - Cut the tomatoes into wedges, slice the cucumber, thinly slice the red onion, and seed and slice the green bell pepper.
     - Place all these vegetables in a large salad bowl.
2. **Add the Olives and Feta:**
     - Add the Kalamata olives (whole or sliced) and crumbled feta cheese to the bowl with the vegetables.
3. **Make the Dressing:**
     - In a small bowl, whisk together the extra virgin olive oil, red wine vinegar, dried oregano, salt, and pepper until well combined.
4. **Combine and Toss:**
     - Pour the dressing over the salad ingredients in the bowl.
     - Gently toss the Greek Salad to coat everything evenly with the dressing.
5. **Serve:**
     - Optional: Garnish with chopped fresh parsley or basil leaves for added freshness and presentation.
     - Serve the Greek Salad immediately as a side dish or as a light and refreshing main course.

Tips:

- For a twist, you can add thinly sliced radishes or pepperoncini peppers to the salad.
- Serve the Greek Salad with crusty bread or pita bread on the side.
- This salad tastes best when served fresh, but leftovers can be stored in an airtight container in the refrigerator for up to 1-2 days.

Enjoy this traditional Greek Salad as a delicious and healthy addition to your meals. It's perfect for summer gatherings, picnics, or anytime you crave a taste of Mediterranean flavors!

Caprese Salad

Ingredients:

- 3-4 ripe tomatoes, preferably vine-ripened or heirloom
- 1 pound fresh mozzarella cheese, sliced into rounds or large chunks
- Fresh basil leaves
- Extra virgin olive oil
- Balsamic glaze (optional)
- Salt and freshly ground black pepper, to taste

Instructions:

1. **Prepare the Tomatoes:**
    - Slice the tomatoes into rounds or thick slices, about 1/4-inch thick. Arrange them on a serving platter or individual plates.
2. **Prepare the Mozzarella:**
    - Slice the fresh mozzarella cheese into rounds or chunks similar in size to the tomato slices. Alternatively, you can use small mozzarella balls (bocconcini).
3. **Assemble the Salad:**
    - Arrange the slices of mozzarella cheese on top of the tomato slices, alternating between tomato and mozzarella for a visually appealing presentation.
4. **Add Basil Leaves:**
    - Place fresh basil leaves between the layers of tomato and mozzarella. You can also tear some basil leaves and scatter them over the salad.
5. **Season and Drizzle:**
    - Season the Caprese Salad with salt and freshly ground black pepper, to taste.
    - Drizzle extra virgin olive oil generously over the salad. Optionally, you can also drizzle balsamic glaze for added sweetness and flavor.
6. **Serve:**
    - Serve the Caprese Salad immediately as an appetizer or a side dish to accompany a main meal.
    - Optionally, garnish with additional basil leaves and a sprinkle of sea salt before serving.

Tips:

- Choose ripe, flavorful tomatoes for the best taste. Heirloom tomatoes or vine-ripened tomatoes are ideal.
- Use fresh, high-quality mozzarella cheese for the authentic Caprese experience. You can use buffalo mozzarella for a richer taste.
- If you prefer a more traditional touch, use whole basil leaves instead of torn ones.

This Caprese Salad is a perfect dish for showcasing the simplicity and freshness of Mediterranean ingredients. It's quick to assemble and makes a delightful addition to any summer meal or gathering. Enjoy the combination of juicy tomatoes, creamy mozzarella, and aromatic basil, drizzled with olive oil and balsamic glaze!

Quinoa Salad with Roasted Vegetables

Ingredients:

- 1 cup quinoa, rinsed
- 2 cups water or vegetable broth
- 1 medium sweet potato, peeled and cut into cubes
- 1 red bell pepper, seeded and sliced
- 1 yellow bell pepper, seeded and sliced
- 1 zucchini, sliced into half moons
- 1 red onion, thinly sliced
- 1 tablespoon olive oil
- Salt and pepper, to taste
- 1/4 cup chopped fresh parsley or cilantro (optional, for garnish)

For the Dressing:

- 1/4 cup extra virgin olive oil
- 2 tablespoons balsamic vinegar
- 1 tablespoon Dijon mustard
- 1 clove garlic, minced
- Salt and pepper, to taste

Instructions:

1. **Prepare the Quinoa:**
    - In a medium saucepan, combine the rinsed quinoa and water or vegetable broth. Bring to a boil, then reduce heat to low, cover, and simmer for 15-20 minutes, or until quinoa is cooked and water is absorbed. Remove from heat and let it sit covered for 5 minutes. Fluff with a fork and transfer to a large mixing bowl to cool.
2. **Roast the Vegetables:**
    - Preheat oven to 400°F (200°C).
    - On a large baking sheet, toss the sweet potato cubes, sliced bell peppers, zucchini slices, and red onion with olive oil, salt, and pepper until evenly coated.
    - Spread the vegetables out in a single layer on the baking sheet.
    - Roast in the preheated oven for 20-25 minutes, stirring halfway through, or until the vegetables are tender and lightly caramelized. Remove from the oven and let cool slightly.

3. **Make the Dressing:**
   - In a small bowl, whisk together the extra virgin olive oil, balsamic vinegar, Dijon mustard, minced garlic, salt, and pepper until well combined.
4. **Assemble the Salad:**
   - Add the roasted vegetables to the cooked quinoa in the mixing bowl.
   - Pour the dressing over the quinoa and roasted vegetables.
   - Toss gently to combine, ensuring the dressing evenly coats the salad ingredients.
5. **Serve:**
   - Garnish with chopped fresh parsley or cilantro, if desired.
   - Serve the Quinoa Salad with Roasted Vegetables warm, at room temperature, or chilled as a nutritious and satisfying main dish or side salad.

Tips:

- Feel free to customize this salad with your favorite roasted vegetables, such as cherry tomatoes, eggplant, or asparagus.
- You can add additional protein by tossing in chickpeas or black beans.
- Store leftovers in an airtight container in the refrigerator for up to 3-4 days. The flavors often meld and improve over time.

This Quinoa Salad with Roasted Vegetables is packed with flavor, texture, and wholesome ingredients, making it a perfect dish for lunch, dinner, or meal prep. Enjoy the combination of fluffy quinoa, tender roasted vegetables, and a tangy dressing in every bite!

Chickpea Salad

Ingredients:

- 2 cans (15 ounces each) chickpeas (garbanzo beans), drained and rinsed
- 1/2 cup cucumber, diced
- 1/2 cup cherry tomatoes, halved
- 1/4 cup red onion, finely chopped
- 1/4 cup fresh parsley, chopped
- 1/4 cup Kalamata olives, pitted and sliced (optional)
- 1/4 cup crumbled feta cheese (optional, omit for vegan)
- Juice of 1 lemon (about 2-3 tablespoons)
- 3 tablespoons extra virgin olive oil
- 1 teaspoon dried oregano
- Salt and pepper, to taste

Instructions:

1. **Prepare the Chickpeas:**
   - Drain and rinse the chickpeas thoroughly under cold water. Place them in a large mixing bowl.
2. **Add Vegetables and Herbs:**
   - Add the diced cucumber, halved cherry tomatoes, finely chopped red onion, chopped fresh parsley, and sliced Kalamata olives (if using) to the bowl with the chickpeas.
3. **Make the Dressing:**
   - In a small bowl, whisk together the lemon juice, extra virgin olive oil, dried oregano, salt, and pepper until well combined.
4. **Combine and Toss:**
   - Pour the dressing over the chickpea and vegetable mixture in the bowl.
   - Toss gently to coat all the ingredients evenly with the dressing.
5. **Optional: Add Feta Cheese (if using):**
   - If using crumbled feta cheese, sprinkle it over the salad and gently toss again.
6. **Serve:**
   - Serve the Chickpea Salad immediately as a side dish, a filling for sandwiches or wraps, or as a light and nutritious main course.

Tips:

- Customize the salad by adding additional vegetables such as bell peppers, diced avocado, or shredded carrots.
- For a creamy texture, mash some of the chickpeas with a fork before adding the dressing.
- This salad can be stored in the refrigerator in an airtight container for up to 3-4 days. Flavors often improve as the salad sits.

Chickpea Salad is not only delicious and easy to prepare but also packed with protein, fiber, and essential nutrients. It's perfect for a quick lunch, a picnic, or as a healthy addition to your meal rotation. Enjoy the fresh and vibrant flavors in every bite!

Beet and Goat Cheese Salad

Ingredients:

- 4 medium-sized beets, preferably red or golden
- 4 cups mixed greens (such as arugula, spinach, or baby greens)
- 1/2 cup crumbled goat cheese
- 1/4 cup walnuts or pecans, toasted and chopped
- 2 tablespoons balsamic vinegar
- 1/4 cup extra virgin olive oil
- 1 teaspoon Dijon mustard
- Salt and freshly ground black pepper, to taste

Instructions:

1. **Roast the Beets:**
    - Preheat the oven to 400°F (200°C).
    - Trim the tops and roots off the beets and scrub them clean. Wrap each beet individually in aluminum foil.
    - Place the wrapped beets on a baking sheet and roast in the preheated oven for 45-60 minutes, or until tender when pierced with a fork.
    - Remove from the oven, let them cool slightly, then peel off the skins using gloves or paper towels (the skins should easily slip off).
2. **Prepare the Vinaigrette:**
    - In a small bowl, whisk together the balsamic vinegar, extra virgin olive oil, Dijon mustard, salt, and pepper until emulsified.
3. **Assemble the Salad:**
    - Slice the roasted beets into rounds or cubes.
    - Arrange the mixed greens on a serving platter or individual plates.
    - Scatter the sliced or cubed roasted beets over the greens.
    - Sprinkle crumbled goat cheese and toasted chopped nuts (walnuts or pecans) over the salad.
4. **Drizzle with Vinaigrette:**
    - Drizzle the prepared balsamic vinaigrette over the Beet and Goat Cheese Salad.
5. **Serve:**
    - Serve the salad immediately as a delicious and colorful appetizer or as a side dish to accompany a main meal.

Tips:

- You can roast the beets ahead of time and store them in the refrigerator until ready to use.
- If you prefer, you can substitute the mixed greens with baby spinach or arugula for a peppery flavor.
- Add a touch of sweetness by sprinkling some dried cranberries or fresh orange segments over the salad.

This Beet and Goat Cheese Salad is a perfect blend of flavors and textures, making it an elegant and satisfying dish for any occasion. Enjoy the combination of earthy beets, creamy goat cheese, crunchy nuts, and tangy vinaigrette in every bite!

Waldorf Salad

Ingredients:

- 2 medium apples, cored and diced (use a variety like Granny Smith or Fuji)
- 1 cup celery, thinly sliced
- 1 cup red seedless grapes, halved
- 1/2 cup walnuts, roughly chopped and toasted
- 1/4 cup raisins or dried cranberries (optional)
- 1/2 cup mayonnaise (or substitute with Greek yogurt for a lighter version)
- 2 tablespoons lemon juice (freshly squeezed)
- 1 tablespoon honey (optional, adjust to taste)
- Salt and freshly ground black pepper, to taste
- Mixed salad greens, for serving (optional)

Instructions:

1. **Prepare the Ingredients:**
   - Core and dice the apples. Thinly slice the celery. Halve the grapes. Roughly chop and toast the walnuts.
2. **Make the Dressing:**
   - In a small bowl, whisk together the mayonnaise (or Greek yogurt), lemon juice, honey (if using), salt, and pepper until well combined. Adjust sweetness and acidity to taste.
3. **Combine the Salad:**
   - In a large mixing bowl, combine the diced apples, sliced celery, halved grapes, toasted walnuts, and optional raisins or dried cranberries.
4. **Add the Dressing:**
   - Pour the dressing over the salad ingredients in the bowl.
   - Gently toss to coat everything evenly with the dressing.
5. **Chill (optional):**
   - For best results, refrigerate the Waldorf Salad for about 30 minutes before serving to allow the flavors to meld.
6. **Serve:**
   - Serve Waldorf Salad on its own or over a bed of mixed salad greens for added freshness and presentation.

Tips:

- To toast the walnuts, spread them out on a baking sheet and toast in a preheated oven at 350°F (175°C) for about 5-7 minutes, or until lightly golden and fragrant. Watch them closely to prevent burning.
- For extra crunch, you can add some finely chopped celery leaves to the salad.
- Adjust the sweetness of the dressing by adding more or less honey, depending on your preference.

Waldorf Salad is a versatile dish that can be enjoyed as a side salad, a light lunch, or a refreshing addition to any meal. It's perfect for gatherings, picnics, or as a delicious way to enjoy seasonal fruits and nuts. Enjoy the crispness of the apples, the crunch of the celery, and the richness of the creamy dressing in this timeless salad!

Mediterranean Orzo Salad

Ingredients:

- 1 cup orzo pasta
- 1/2 cup Kalamata olives, pitted and sliced
- 1/2 cup sun-dried tomatoes, chopped (packed in oil and drained)
- 1/2 cup cucumber, diced
- 1/4 cup red onion, finely chopped
- 1/4 cup fresh parsley, chopped
- 1/4 cup fresh basil leaves, chopped
- 1/2 cup crumbled feta cheese
- 1/4 cup pine nuts or toasted almonds (optional, for extra crunch)
- Juice of 1 lemon (about 2-3 tablespoons)
- 1/4 cup extra virgin olive oil
- 1 clove garlic, minced
- Salt and freshly ground black pepper, to taste

Instructions:

1. **Cook the Orzo:**
    - Cook the orzo pasta according to package instructions until al dente. Drain and rinse under cold water to stop the cooking process. Drain well and transfer to a large mixing bowl.
2. **Prepare the Ingredients:**
    - Pit and slice the Kalamata olives. Chop the sun-dried tomatoes (if they are not already chopped). Dice the cucumber, finely chop the red onion, and chop the fresh parsley and basil leaves.
3. **Make the Dressing:**
    - In a small bowl, whisk together the lemon juice, extra virgin olive oil, minced garlic, salt, and pepper until well combined.
4. **Assemble the Salad:**
    - Add the sliced Kalamata olives, chopped sun-dried tomatoes, diced cucumber, finely chopped red onion, chopped fresh parsley, chopped fresh basil, and crumbled feta cheese to the bowl with the cooked orzo.
5. **Add the Dressing:**
    - Pour the prepared dressing over the salad ingredients in the bowl.
6. **Toss and Chill:**
    - Gently toss all the ingredients together until evenly coated with the dressing.

- For best flavor, refrigerate the Mediterranean Orzo Salad for at least 30 minutes before serving to allow the flavors to meld.
7. **Serve:**
    - Optional: Sprinkle toasted pine nuts or almonds over the salad before serving for extra crunch and flavor.
    - Serve the Mediterranean Orzo Salad chilled or at room temperature as a delicious side dish or a light and satisfying main course.

Tips:

- Customize the salad by adding ingredients like artichoke hearts, roasted bell peppers, or cherry tomatoes.
- If making ahead of time, you may need to refresh the salad with a little extra dressing before serving, as the orzo can absorb some of the moisture.
- This salad can be stored in the refrigerator in an airtight container for up to 3-4 days. It's perfect for meal prep or enjoying as leftovers.

Enjoy the fresh Mediterranean flavors and textures in this delightful Orzo Salad! It's perfect for summer gatherings, potlucks, or anytime you crave a taste of the Mediterranean cuisine.

Thai Papaya Salad (Som Tum)

Ingredients:

- 1 medium green papaya (about 2 cups), peeled and julienned
- 1-2 cloves garlic, minced
- 2-3 Thai bird's eye chilies, finely chopped (adjust to taste)
- 1-2 tablespoons dried shrimp (optional, omit for vegetarian/vegan)
- 2 tablespoons roasted peanuts, coarsely chopped
- 1-2 tablespoons fish sauce (or soy sauce for vegetarian/vegan)
- 1-2 tablespoons palm sugar or brown sugar
- 2 tablespoons fresh lime juice
- 1-2 tablespoons tamarind paste (optional, for tanginess)
- 1 cup cherry tomatoes, halved
- 1/4 cup long beans or green beans, cut into 1-inch pieces (optional)
- 1/4 cup carrots, julienned (optional)
- Fresh cilantro leaves, for garnish
- Fresh Thai basil leaves, for garnish (optional)

Instructions:

1. **Prepare the Green Papaya:**
    - Peel the green papaya and cut it into thin matchstick-like strips using a julienne peeler or a sharp knife. Place the julienned papaya in a large mixing bowl.
2. **Make the Dressing:**
    - In a mortar and pestle, pound the minced garlic and chopped Thai chilies together until they form a rough paste. Add dried shrimp (if using) and lightly crush them.
    - Add fish sauce (or soy sauce), palm sugar (or brown sugar), lime juice, and tamarind paste (if using). Adjust the seasoning to balance the flavors of salty, sweet, sour, and spicy.
3. **Combine Ingredients:**
    - Add the halved cherry tomatoes, chopped peanuts, long beans (or green beans), and julienned carrots (if using) to the bowl with the julienned papaya.
4. **Toss the Salad:**
    - Pour the prepared dressing over the salad ingredients in the bowl.
    - Toss everything together gently but thoroughly to ensure all the ingredients are coated with the dressing.

5. **Serve:**
    - Transfer the Thai Papaya Salad to a serving platter or individual plates.
    - Garnish with fresh cilantro leaves and Thai basil leaves (if using).
    - Serve immediately as a refreshing appetizer or side dish to accompany Thai meals.

Tips:

- Adjust the level of spiciness by adding more or fewer Thai bird's eye chilies.
- If you prefer a milder salad, deseed the Thai chilies before chopping.
- For a vegetarian or vegan version, omit the dried shrimp and use soy sauce instead of fish sauce.
- Green papaya can be found in Asian grocery stores. If unavailable, you can substitute with green mango or even cucumber for a different texture.

Thai Papaya Salad (Som Tum) is a perfect blend of spicy, sweet, tangy, and crunchy flavors, making it a favorite among Thai cuisine lovers. Enjoy the vibrant colors and fresh ingredients in this traditional Thai salad!

Caesar Salad with Homemade Dressing

Ingredients:

For the Salad:

- 1 head of romaine lettuce, washed, dried, and torn into bite-sized pieces
- 1 cup croutons (store-bought or homemade)
- 1/2 cup shaved or grated Parmesan cheese

For the Dressing:

- 1/2 cup mayonnaise
- 1/4 cup grated Parmesan cheese
- 2 tablespoons fresh lemon juice
- 1 tablespoon Dijon mustard
- 1 clove garlic, minced
- 1 anchovy fillet, minced (optional, for traditional Caesar dressing)
- 1/2 teaspoon Worcestershire sauce
- Salt and freshly ground black pepper, to taste
- 2-3 tablespoons extra virgin olive oil (optional, for a thinner dressing)

Instructions:

1. **Make the Dressing:**
   - In a small bowl, whisk together the mayonnaise, grated Parmesan cheese, fresh lemon juice, Dijon mustard, minced garlic, anchovy fillet (if using), Worcestershire sauce, salt, and pepper until well combined.
   - Optional: For a thinner dressing, gradually whisk in extra virgin olive oil until desired consistency is reached. Taste and adjust seasoning if needed.
2. **Prepare the Salad:**
   - In a large salad bowl, add the torn romaine lettuce leaves.
   - Add the croutons on top of the lettuce.
3. **Assemble the Salad:**
   - Drizzle the homemade Caesar dressing over the salad.
   - Toss gently to coat the lettuce and croutons evenly with the dressing.
4. **Add Parmesan Cheese:**
   - Sprinkle shaved or grated Parmesan cheese over the salad.
5. **Serve:**

- Serve the Caesar Salad immediately as a side dish or add grilled chicken or shrimp to make it a main course.

Tips:

- For homemade croutons, cube stale bread, toss with olive oil, salt, and pepper, and bake at 375°F (190°C) for about 10-15 minutes until golden and crispy.
- Adjust the amount of lemon juice and garlic in the dressing according to your taste preferences.
- If you prefer a vegetarian version, omit the anchovy fillet or use anchovy paste for a milder flavor.
- Store any leftover dressing in an airtight container in the refrigerator for up to 3-4 days.

Enjoy the classic flavors of Caesar Salad with this homemade dressing recipe. It's perfect for a light lunch, a side dish at dinner, or as part of a buffet spread for gatherings!

Spinach and Strawberry Salad

Ingredients:

For the Salad:

- 6 cups baby spinach leaves, washed and dried
- 1 pint strawberries, hulled and sliced
- 1/2 cup sliced almonds or chopped pecans
- 1/4 cup crumbled feta cheese or goat cheese (optional)

For the Dressing:

- 1/4 cup extra virgin olive oil
- 2 tablespoons balsamic vinegar
- 1 tablespoon honey or maple syrup
- 1 teaspoon Dijon mustard
- Salt and freshly ground black pepper, to taste

Instructions:

1. **Prepare the Dressing:**
   - In a small bowl, whisk together the extra virgin olive oil, balsamic vinegar, honey (or maple syrup), Dijon mustard, salt, and pepper until well combined. Adjust sweetness and acidity to taste.
2. **Assemble the Salad:**
   - In a large salad bowl, combine the baby spinach leaves, sliced strawberries, and sliced almonds or chopped pecans.
3. **Add Optional Cheese:**
   - If using, sprinkle crumbled feta cheese or goat cheese over the salad ingredients.
4. **Toss with Dressing:**
   - Drizzle the prepared dressing over the salad.
5. **Toss Gently:**
   - Toss the Spinach and Strawberry Salad gently to evenly coat the ingredients with the dressing.
6. **Serve:**
   - Serve the salad immediately as a refreshing side dish or light lunch.

Tips:

- For added protein, you can add grilled chicken or shrimp to make this salad a more substantial meal.
- Feel free to customize the salad with additional ingredients like avocado slices, red onion, or dried cranberries.
- To toast the almonds or pecans, spread them in a single layer on a baking sheet and bake at 350°F (175°C) for about 5-7 minutes, or until lightly golden and fragrant. Watch them closely to prevent burning.
- This salad can be stored in the refrigerator without dressing for up to a day. Add dressing just before serving to keep the salad fresh and crisp.

Spinach and Strawberry Salad is not only delicious but also packed with vitamins, antioxidants, and fiber. It's perfect for spring and summer gatherings or as a healthy addition to your weekly meal plan. Enjoy the combination of sweet strawberries, crunchy nuts, and tangy dressing in every bite!

Mexican Street Corn Salad (Esquites)

Ingredients:

- 4 cups corn kernels (about 4-5 ears of corn)
- 2 tablespoons mayonnaise
- 2 tablespoons sour cream or Mexican crema
- 1/2 cup crumbled cotija cheese (or feta cheese)
- 1/4 cup finely chopped fresh cilantro
- 1-2 cloves garlic, minced
- 1 jalapeño, seeded and finely chopped (optional, for heat)
- Juice of 1 lime (about 2 tablespoons)
- 1 teaspoon chili powder (adjust to taste)
- Salt and freshly ground black pepper, to taste
- Lime wedges, for serving
- Tortilla chips or tostadas, for serving (optional)

Instructions:

1. **Cook the Corn:**
   - If using fresh corn on the cob, grill or boil the corn until cooked through. Let it cool, then cut the kernels off the cob. Alternatively, you can use frozen corn kernels, thawed and drained.
2. **Prepare the Dressing:**
   - In a large bowl, combine the mayonnaise, sour cream or Mexican crema, minced garlic, chopped jalapeño (if using), lime juice, chili powder, salt, and pepper. Whisk until smooth and well combined.
3. **Assemble the Salad:**
   - Add the corn kernels to the bowl with the dressing.
   - Gently fold in the crumbled cotija cheese (or feta cheese) and chopped cilantro until evenly distributed and coated with the dressing.
4. **Chill (Optional):**
   - For best flavor, refrigerate the Mexican Street Corn Salad for at least 30 minutes before serving to allow the flavors to meld.
5. **Serve:**
   - Serve the Esquites salad cold or at room temperature.
   - Garnish with additional crumbled cotija cheese, chopped cilantro, a sprinkle of chili powder, and lime wedges on the side.
6. **Optional Serving Suggestions:**

- Serve with tortilla chips or tostadas for scooping up the salad, or as a side dish to grilled meats or tacos.

Tips:

- If you prefer a smokier flavor, you can char the corn kernels on a grill or under a broiler before assembling the salad.
- Adjust the amount of chili powder and jalapeño according to your preferred level of spiciness.
- If cotija cheese is not available, feta cheese makes a good substitute with a similar salty flavor.

Mexican Street Corn Salad (Esquites) is a perfect blend of creamy, tangy, and slightly spicy flavors, making it a popular dish for summer parties, barbecues, or any Mexican-inspired meal. Enjoy the taste of elote in this convenient and delicious salad form!

Kale Salad with Lemon Tahini Dressing

Ingredients:

For the Salad:

- 1 bunch kale (about 6 cups), tough stems removed and leaves chopped
- 1 cup cherry tomatoes, halved
- 1/2 cucumber, sliced
- 1/4 cup red onion, thinly sliced
- 1/4 cup toasted sunflower seeds or pepitas (pumpkin seeds)
- Optional: 1/4 cup crumbled feta cheese or goat cheese

For the Lemon Tahini Dressing:

- 1/4 cup tahini (sesame seed paste)
- Juice of 1 lemon (about 2-3 tablespoons)
- 2 tablespoons extra virgin olive oil
- 1-2 cloves garlic, minced
- 1 tablespoon maple syrup or honey (optional, for sweetness)
- 2-4 tablespoons water, to thin the dressing
- Salt and freshly ground black pepper, to taste

Instructions:

1. **Prepare the Kale:**
   - Remove the tough stems from the kale leaves and chop or tear the leaves into bite-sized pieces. Place them in a large salad bowl.
2. **Make the Lemon Tahini Dressing:**
   - In a small bowl, whisk together the tahini, lemon juice, extra virgin olive oil, minced garlic, maple syrup or honey (if using), salt, and pepper until smooth.
   - Gradually whisk in water, 1 tablespoon at a time, until the dressing reaches a pourable consistency.
3. **Massage the Kale:**
   - Pour about half of the Lemon Tahini Dressing over the kale leaves.
   - Using clean hands, massage the dressing into the kale leaves for 2-3 minutes until the kale begins to soften and wilt slightly.
4. **Assemble the Salad:**
   - Add the halved cherry tomatoes, sliced cucumber, thinly sliced red onion, and toasted sunflower seeds or pepitas to the bowl with the kale.

5. **Toss with Remaining Dressing:**
   - Drizzle the remaining Lemon Tahini Dressing over the salad ingredients.
   - Toss gently to coat everything evenly with the dressing.
6. **Optional: Add Cheese**
   - If using, sprinkle crumbled feta cheese or goat cheese over the salad before serving.
7. **Serve:**
   - Serve the Kale Salad with Lemon Tahini Dressing immediately as a nutritious and flavorful side dish or add grilled chicken or tofu to make it a satisfying main course.

Tips:

- To toast sunflower seeds or pepitas, heat them in a dry skillet over medium heat, stirring frequently, until lightly golden and fragrant.
- The massaging process helps to tenderize the kale leaves and enhance their flavor.
- Adjust the sweetness and tanginess of the dressing by adding more or less lemon juice and maple syrup or honey.
- This salad can be stored in the refrigerator in an airtight container for up to 2-3 days. The flavors often meld together nicely after marinating for a while.

Enjoy the nutrient-packed goodness of Kale Salad with Lemon Tahini Dressing, perfect for a healthy lunch, light dinner, or as a side dish for any occasion!

Watermelon Feta Salad

Ingredients:

- 4 cups cubed seedless watermelon
- 1/2 cup crumbled feta cheese
- 1/4 cup fresh mint leaves, thinly sliced or chopped
- 1/4 cup red onion, thinly sliced (optional, for a bit of bite)
- 1/4 cup sliced almonds or toasted pine nuts (optional, for added crunch)

For the Vinaigrette:

- 2 tablespoons extra virgin olive oil
- 1 tablespoon balsamic vinegar (or red wine vinegar)
- 1 teaspoon honey or maple syrup
- Salt and freshly ground black pepper, to taste

Instructions:

1. **Prepare the Watermelon:**
    - Cut the watermelon into bite-sized cubes. Place them in a large salad bowl.
2. **Make the Vinaigrette:**
    - In a small bowl, whisk together the extra virgin olive oil, balsamic vinegar, honey or maple syrup, salt, and pepper until well combined.
3. **Assemble the Salad:**
    - Add the crumbled feta cheese, thinly sliced fresh mint leaves, and optional red onion slices to the bowl with the watermelon.
4. **Drizzle with Vinaigrette:**
    - Pour the prepared vinaigrette over the salad ingredients.
5. **Gently Toss:**
    - Gently toss all the ingredients together until evenly coated with the vinaigrette.
6. **Optional: Add Nuts**
    - If using, sprinkle sliced almonds or toasted pine nuts over the Watermelon Feta Salad for added crunch and flavor.
7. **Serve:**
    - Serve the salad immediately as a refreshing side dish or as a light and healthy summer appetizer.

Tips:

- For best results, assemble the salad just before serving to maintain the crispness of the watermelon.
- Customize the salad by adding sliced cucumber or arugula for extra freshness.
- Adjust the sweetness of the vinaigrette by adding more or less honey or maple syrup, depending on your preference.
- This salad pairs well with grilled meats, seafood, or as a part of a picnic or barbecue spread.

Watermelon Feta Salad is a delightful blend of sweet and savory flavors with a burst of freshness from the mint, making it perfect for summer gatherings or any occasion when you want a light and refreshing salad. Enjoy the contrast of flavors and textures in every bite!

Lentil Salad with Roasted Vegetables

Ingredients:

For the Salad:

- 1 cup green or brown lentils, rinsed
- 3 cups water or vegetable broth
- 2 cups mixed vegetables (such as bell peppers, zucchini, cherry tomatoes, red onion, etc.), chopped into bite-sized pieces
- 2 tablespoons olive oil
- Salt and freshly ground black pepper, to taste
- 1/4 cup chopped fresh herbs (such as parsley, basil, or cilantro)

For the Dressing:

- 3 tablespoons extra virgin olive oil
- 2 tablespoons balsamic vinegar
- 1 tablespoon Dijon mustard
- 1 clove garlic, minced
- Salt and freshly ground black pepper, to taste

Instructions:

1. **Roast the Vegetables:**
    - Preheat the oven to 400°F (200°C).
    - In a large bowl, toss the chopped vegetables with 2 tablespoons of olive oil, salt, and pepper until evenly coated.
    - Spread the vegetables in a single layer on a baking sheet.
    - Roast in the preheated oven for 20-25 minutes, or until the vegetables are tender and lightly caramelized, stirring halfway through. Remove from the oven and let cool slightly.
2. **Cook the Lentils:**
    - In a medium saucepan, combine the rinsed lentils and water or vegetable broth. Bring to a boil over medium-high heat.
    - Reduce the heat to low, cover, and simmer for 15-20 minutes, or until the lentils are tender but still hold their shape. Drain any excess liquid and let cool.
3. **Make the Dressing:**
    - In a small bowl, whisk together the extra virgin olive oil, balsamic vinegar, Dijon mustard, minced garlic, salt, and pepper until well combined.

4. **Assemble the Salad:**
   - In a large salad bowl, combine the cooked lentils, roasted vegetables, and chopped fresh herbs.
   - Drizzle the dressing over the salad ingredients.
5. **Toss Gently:**
   - Gently toss the Lentil Salad with Roasted Vegetables until everything is evenly coated with the dressing.
6. **Serve:**
   - Serve the salad warm, at room temperature, or chilled.
   - Garnish with additional fresh herbs if desired.

Tips:

- You can use any combination of vegetables for roasting, depending on your preference and seasonal availability.
- To add more flavor, you can sprinkle crumbled feta cheese or goat cheese over the salad before serving.
- This salad can be made ahead of time and stored in the refrigerator for up to 3 days. The flavors often meld together nicely after marinating for a while.

Enjoy this hearty and flavorful Lentil Salad with Roasted Vegetables as a satisfying main dish or a nutritious side dish. It's perfect for meal prep, picnics, potlucks, or any occasion where you want a wholesome and delicious salad!

Tabouli Salad

Ingredients:

- 1 cup bulgur wheat
- 1 1/2 cups boiling water
- 1/4 cup extra virgin olive oil
- Juice of 2-3 lemons (about 1/2 cup)
- 2 cups fresh parsley leaves, finely chopped
- 1/2 cup fresh mint leaves, finely chopped
- 2-3 medium tomatoes, finely diced
- 1/2 cucumber, finely diced
- 1/4 cup red onion or green onion, finely chopped
- Salt and freshly ground black pepper, to taste

Instructions:

1. **Prepare the Bulgur Wheat:**
   - Place the bulgur wheat in a heatproof bowl.
   - Pour the boiling water over the bulgur wheat, cover with a plate or plastic wrap, and let it sit for about 20-30 minutes, or until the bulgur is tender and has absorbed all the water. Fluff with a fork and let it cool.
2. **Make the Dressing:**
   - In a small bowl, whisk together the extra virgin olive oil and lemon juice until well combined. Season with salt and pepper to taste.
3. **Combine Ingredients:**
   - In a large salad bowl, combine the cooled bulgur wheat, chopped parsley, chopped mint, diced tomatoes, diced cucumber, and chopped onion.
4. **Add Dressing:**
   - Pour the dressing over the salad ingredients.
5. **Toss Gently:**
   - Gently toss all the ingredients together until evenly coated with the dressing.
6. **Chill (Optional):**
   - For best flavor, refrigerate the Tabouli Salad for at least 1 hour before serving to allow the flavors to meld together.
7. **Serve:**
   - Serve the Tabouli Salad chilled or at room temperature as a refreshing side dish or light lunch.

Tips:

- Adjust the amount of lemon juice and olive oil in the dressing according to your taste preferences.
- Tabouli is traditionally served with lettuce leaves or pita bread, making it versatile for different serving styles.
- For a gluten-free version, you can substitute quinoa for bulgur wheat.
- Customize your Tabouli Salad by adding chopped olives, bell peppers, or a sprinkle of sumac for extra flavor.

Tabouli Salad is a nutritious and flavorful dish that's perfect for summer picnics, barbecues, or as a healthy addition to any Mediterranean-inspired meal. Enjoy the fresh and tangy flavors in every bite!

Asian Slaw

Ingredients:

For the Slaw:

- 4 cups shredded cabbage (green, purple, or a mix)
- 1 cup shredded carrots
- 1 cup shredded red cabbage
- 1 bell pepper (any color), thinly sliced
- 1/2 cup chopped fresh cilantro or parsley
- 1/4 cup chopped green onions (scallions)
- 1/4 cup toasted sesame seeds (optional, for garnish)

For the Dressing:

- 1/4 cup soy sauce or tamari (for gluten-free option)
- 2 tablespoons rice vinegar
- 1 tablespoon sesame oil
- 1 tablespoon honey or maple syrup
- 1 tablespoon fresh ginger, grated
- 1 clove garlic, minced
- 1/4 teaspoon red pepper flakes (optional, for heat)
- Salt and freshly ground black pepper, to taste

Instructions:

1. **Prepare the Vegetables:**
    - In a large bowl, combine the shredded cabbage, shredded carrots, shredded red cabbage, sliced bell pepper, chopped cilantro or parsley, and chopped green onions.
2. **Make the Dressing:**
    - In a small bowl or jar, whisk together the soy sauce or tamari, rice vinegar, sesame oil, honey or maple syrup, grated ginger, minced garlic, red pepper flakes (if using), salt, and pepper until well combined.
3. **Combine Slaw with Dressing:**
    - Pour the dressing over the slaw ingredients.
4. **Toss Gently:**
    - Toss the Asian Slaw gently until all the vegetables are evenly coated with the dressing.
5. **Chill (Optional):**

- For best flavor, refrigerate the Asian Slaw for at least 30 minutes before serving to allow the flavors to meld together.
6. **Serve:**
    - Serve the Asian Slaw chilled as a refreshing side dish or as a crunchy topping for sandwiches, tacos, or wraps.
    - Garnish with toasted sesame seeds before serving, if desired.

Tips:

- Feel free to customize the slaw by adding other vegetables such as shredded broccoli, snow peas, or bean sprouts.
- Adjust the sweetness and tanginess of the dressing by varying the amount of honey or vinegar to suit your taste.
- This slaw can be stored in the refrigerator in an airtight container for up to 3 days. The flavors often develop more after marinating for a while.

Asian Slaw is a colorful and nutritious addition to any meal, offering a delightful blend of textures and flavors with a hint of Asian-inspired dressing. Enjoy it as a side dish, a light lunch, or a topping for various dishes!

Avocado and Tomato Salad

Ingredients:

- 2 ripe avocados, peeled, pitted, and diced
- 2 large tomatoes, diced (use vine-ripened or Roma tomatoes for best flavor)
- 1/4 cup red onion, finely chopped (optional, for added bite)
- 1/4 cup fresh cilantro or parsley, chopped
- Juice of 1 lime (about 2 tablespoons)
- 2 tablespoons extra virgin olive oil
- Salt and freshly ground black pepper, to taste

Instructions:

1. **Prepare the Ingredients:**
   - Dice the avocados and tomatoes into bite-sized pieces.
   - Finely chop the red onion (if using) and fresh cilantro or parsley.
2. **Assemble the Salad:**
   - In a large salad bowl, combine the diced avocados, diced tomatoes, chopped red onion (if using), and chopped cilantro or parsley.
3. **Make the Dressing:**
   - In a small bowl, whisk together the lime juice, extra virgin olive oil, salt, and pepper until well combined.
4. **Drizzle and Toss:**
   - Pour the dressing over the avocado and tomato mixture.
5. **Gently Toss:**
   - Gently toss all the ingredients together until evenly coated with the dressing.
6. **Serve:**
   - Serve the Avocado and Tomato Salad immediately as a refreshing side dish or a light lunch.

Tips:

- To prevent the avocados from browning, toss them gently with the lime juice and dressing just before serving.
- Customize your salad by adding other ingredients such as cucumber, bell peppers, or a sprinkle of crumbled feta cheese.
- Adjust the seasoning and acidity of the dressing to suit your taste preferences.

Avocado and Tomato Salad is perfect for summer gatherings, picnics, or as a healthy addition to any meal. Enjoy the combination of creamy avocado and juicy tomatoes with a zesty lime dressing in every bite!

Roasted Cauliflower Salad

Ingredients:

For the Roasted Cauliflower:

- 1 head cauliflower, cut into florets
- 2 tablespoons olive oil
- 1 teaspoon ground cumin
- 1 teaspoon smoked paprika
- Salt and freshly ground black pepper, to taste

For the Salad:

- 4 cups mixed greens (such as spinach, arugula, or lettuce)
- 1/2 cup cherry tomatoes, halved
- 1/4 cup red onion, thinly sliced
- 1/4 cup fresh parsley or cilantro, chopped
- 1/4 cup toasted almonds or pine nuts
- Optional: 1/4 cup crumbled feta cheese or goat cheese

For the Dressing:

- 3 tablespoons extra virgin olive oil
- 2 tablespoons balsamic vinegar
- 1 tablespoon Dijon mustard
- 1 clove garlic, minced
- Salt and freshly ground black pepper, to taste

Instructions:

1. **Roast the Cauliflower:**
    - Preheat the oven to 425°F (220°C).
    - In a large bowl, toss the cauliflower florets with olive oil, ground cumin, smoked paprika, salt, and pepper until evenly coated.
    - Spread the cauliflower in a single layer on a baking sheet.
    - Roast in the preheated oven for 20-25 minutes, or until the cauliflower is golden brown and tender, stirring halfway through. Remove from the oven and let cool slightly.
2. **Make the Dressing:**

- In a small bowl, whisk together the extra virgin olive oil, balsamic vinegar, Dijon mustard, minced garlic, salt, and pepper until well combined.
3. **Assemble the Salad:**
    - In a large salad bowl, combine the mixed greens, roasted cauliflower florets, cherry tomatoes, thinly sliced red onion, chopped parsley or cilantro, and toasted almonds or pine nuts.
4. **Add Optional Cheese:**
    - If using, sprinkle crumbled feta cheese or goat cheese over the salad ingredients.
5. **Drizzle with Dressing:**
    - Pour the dressing over the salad.
6. **Toss Gently:**
    - Gently toss all the ingredients together until evenly coated with the dressing.
7. **Serve:**
    - Serve the Roasted Cauliflower Salad immediately as a nutritious and flavorful side dish or light lunch.

Tips:

- Customize the salad by adding other vegetables such as bell peppers or cucumber.
- To toast almonds or pine nuts, heat them in a dry skillet over medium heat, stirring frequently, until lightly golden and fragrant.
- This salad can be stored in the refrigerator in an airtight container for up to 2-3 days. Add the dressing just before serving to keep the salad fresh and crisp.

Roasted Cauliflower Salad is a delicious and wholesome dish that combines the earthy flavor of roasted cauliflower with fresh greens, nuts, and a tangy dressing. Enjoy the contrast of textures and flavors in every bite!

Pasta Salad with Pesto

Ingredients:

For the Salad:

- 8 ounces (about 225g) pasta of your choice (penne, fusilli, or rotini work well)
- 1 cup cherry tomatoes, halved
- 1/2 cup black olives, sliced
- 1/2 cup red bell pepper, diced
- 1/4 cup red onion, finely chopped
- 1/4 cup fresh basil leaves, chopped
- Optional: 1/4 cup crumbled feta cheese or grated Parmesan cheese

For the Pesto:

- 2 cups fresh basil leaves, packed
- 1/2 cup grated Parmesan cheese
- 1/2 cup pine nuts or walnuts
- 2 garlic cloves, minced
- 1/2 cup extra virgin olive oil
- Salt and freshly ground black pepper, to taste

Instructions:

1. **Cook the Pasta:**
    - Cook the pasta according to the package instructions until al dente. Drain and rinse under cold water to stop the cooking process. Let it cool.
2. **Make the Pesto:**
    - In a food processor, combine the basil leaves, grated Parmesan cheese, pine nuts or walnuts, and minced garlic.
    - Pulse until finely chopped.
    - With the food processor running, gradually add the olive oil in a steady stream until the pesto reaches a smooth consistency. Scrape down the sides of the processor as needed.
    - Season with salt and pepper to taste.
3. **Assemble the Salad:**
    - In a large bowl, combine the cooled pasta, halved cherry tomatoes, sliced black olives, diced red bell pepper, finely chopped red onion, and chopped fresh basil leaves.
4. **Add Pesto:**

    - Add the prepared pesto to the pasta salad.
5. **Toss Gently:**
    - Gently toss all the ingredients together until the pasta and vegetables are evenly coated with the pesto.
6. **Add Optional Cheese:**
    - If using, sprinkle crumbled feta cheese or grated Parmesan cheese over the salad.
7. **Chill (Optional):**
    - For best flavor, refrigerate the Pasta Salad with Pesto for at least 30 minutes before serving to allow the flavors to meld together.
8. **Serve:**
    - Serve the Pasta Salad with Pesto chilled or at room temperature as a delicious side dish or a light main course.

Tips:

- You can customize the pasta salad by adding grilled chicken, shrimp, or roasted vegetables for extra protein and flavor.
- Store any leftover pesto in an airtight container in the refrigerator for up to 1 week or freeze it for longer storage.
- Adjust the consistency of the pesto by adding more olive oil if desired.

Pasta Salad with Pesto is a versatile and satisfying dish that's perfect for picnics, potlucks, or as a refreshing summer meal. Enjoy the fresh flavors of basil pesto combined with pasta and vegetables in every bite!

Moroccan Carrot Salad

Ingredients:

For the Salad:

- 1 lb (about 450g) carrots, peeled and sliced into rounds or matchsticks
- 1/4 cup golden raisins or chopped dates
- 1/4 cup chopped fresh parsley or cilantro
- 1/4 cup chopped almonds or pistachios, toasted
- Optional: 1/4 cup crumbled feta cheese or goat cheese

For the Dressing:

- 3 tablespoons extra virgin olive oil
- Juice of 1 lemon (about 2-3 tablespoons)
- 1 teaspoon ground cumin
- 1/2 teaspoon ground cinnamon
- 1/2 teaspoon paprika
- 1/4 teaspoon ground ginger
- Pinch of cayenne pepper (optional, for heat)
- Salt and freshly ground black pepper, to taste

Instructions:

1. **Cook the Carrots:**
   - Bring a pot of water to a boil. Add the sliced carrots and cook for about 5-7 minutes, or until tender but still slightly crisp (al dente). Drain the carrots and let them cool.
2. **Prepare the Dressing:**
   - In a small bowl, whisk together the extra virgin olive oil, lemon juice, ground cumin, ground cinnamon, paprika, ground ginger, cayenne pepper (if using), salt, and pepper until well combined.
3. **Assemble the Salad:**
   - In a large salad bowl, combine the cooked and cooled carrots, golden raisins or chopped dates, chopped fresh parsley or cilantro, and toasted almonds or pistachios.
4. **Add Dressing:**
   - Pour the dressing over the salad ingredients.
5. **Toss Gently:**

- Gently toss all the ingredients together until the carrots and other ingredients are evenly coated with the dressing.
6. **Add Optional Cheese:**
    - If using, sprinkle crumbled feta cheese or goat cheese over the salad.
7. **Chill (Optional):**
    - For best flavor, refrigerate the Moroccan Carrot Salad for at least 30 minutes before serving to allow the flavors to meld together.
8. **Serve:**
    - Serve the Moroccan Carrot Salad chilled or at room temperature as a flavorful side dish or light lunch.

Tips:

- Adjust the spices and seasonings in the dressing according to your taste preferences. Moroccan cuisine often balances sweet, savory, and spicy flavors.
- For added sweetness, you can drizzle a little honey or maple syrup into the dressing.
- This salad can be made ahead of time and stored in the refrigerator in an airtight container for up to 3 days.

Moroccan Carrot Salad is a delicious and exotic dish that offers a delightful blend of textures and flavors. Enjoy the aromatic spices and nutty crunch combined with the sweetness of carrots and raisins in every bite!

Potato Salad with Dill Dressing

Ingredients:

For the Potato Salad:

- 2 lbs (about 1 kg) potatoes (preferably Yukon Gold or red potatoes), peeled and cut into bite-sized pieces
- 1/2 cup celery, finely chopped
- 1/4 cup red onion, finely chopped
- 1/4 cup fresh dill, chopped
- Optional: 1/4 cup chopped fresh parsley
- Salt and freshly ground black pepper, to taste

For the Dressing:

- 1 cup mayonnaise (you can use reduced-fat or vegan mayo)
- 2 tablespoons Dijon mustard
- 2 tablespoons apple cider vinegar or white vinegar
- 1 tablespoon fresh lemon juice
- 1-2 cloves garlic, minced
- 2 tablespoons fresh dill, chopped
- Salt and freshly ground black pepper, to taste

Instructions:

1. **Cook the Potatoes:**
   - Place the peeled and diced potatoes in a large pot and cover with cold water. Add a pinch of salt.
   - Bring to a boil over medium-high heat. Reduce the heat to medium-low and simmer for about 10-15 minutes, or until the potatoes are tender when pierced with a fork.
   - Drain the potatoes and let them cool slightly.
2. **Prepare the Dressing:**
   - In a large mixing bowl, whisk together the mayonnaise, Dijon mustard, apple cider vinegar, fresh lemon juice, minced garlic, chopped dill, salt, and pepper until smooth and well combined.
3. **Assemble the Salad:**
   - Add the cooked and slightly cooled potatoes to the bowl with the dressing.
   - Add the chopped celery, finely chopped red onion, fresh dill, and optional chopped parsley.

- Gently toss all the ingredients together until the potatoes and vegetables are evenly coated with the dressing.
4. **Chill (Optional):**
    - For best flavor, refrigerate the Potato Salad with Dill Dressing for at least 1 hour before serving to allow the flavors to meld together.
5. **Serve:**
    - Serve the Potato Salad chilled or at room temperature as a delicious side dish or a light meal.

Tips:

- Adjust the amount of mayonnaise and mustard to achieve your desired creaminess and tanginess.
- For a lighter version, you can use Greek yogurt or a combination of yogurt and mayonnaise in place of all mayo.
- Add chopped hard-boiled eggs for extra protein and flavor, if desired.
- This salad can be made ahead of time and stored in the refrigerator in an airtight container for up to 3 days.

Potato Salad with Dill Dressing is a comforting and versatile dish that's perfect for picnics, barbecues, potlucks, or as a side dish for any occasion. Enjoy the creamy texture of the potatoes combined with the freshness of dill and herbs in every bite!

Cucumber Salad with Yogurt Dressing

Ingredients:

For the Salad:

- 2 large cucumbers, thinly sliced (preferably English cucumbers)
- 1/4 red onion, thinly sliced (optional, for added flavor)
- 1/4 cup fresh dill, chopped (or use parsley if preferred)
- Salt and freshly ground black pepper, to taste

For the Yogurt Dressing:

- 1 cup plain Greek yogurt (or regular yogurt)
- 1-2 tablespoons fresh lemon juice
- 1 tablespoon extra virgin olive oil
- 1 clove garlic, minced (optional, for added flavor)
- 1 tablespoon chopped fresh dill (or parsley)
- Salt and freshly ground black pepper, to taste

Instructions:

1. **Prepare the Dressing:**
   - In a small bowl, whisk together the Greek yogurt, fresh lemon juice, extra virgin olive oil, minced garlic (if using), chopped dill or parsley, salt, and pepper until smooth and well combined. Adjust the lemon juice, salt, and pepper to taste.
2. **Assemble the Salad:**
   - In a large salad bowl, combine the thinly sliced cucumbers and red onion (if using).
3. **Add the Dressing:**
   - Pour the yogurt dressing over the cucumber and onion mixture.
4. **Toss Gently:**
   - Gently toss all the ingredients together until the cucumbers and onion slices are evenly coated with the yogurt dressing.
5. **Chill (Optional):**
   - For best flavor, refrigerate the Cucumber Salad with Yogurt Dressing for at least 30 minutes before serving to allow the flavors to meld together.
6. **Serve:**
   - Serve the Cucumber Salad chilled as a refreshing side dish or a light lunch.

Tips:

- If using regular yogurt instead of Greek yogurt, you might need to strain it for a thicker consistency.
- Add a pinch of sugar or honey to the dressing if you prefer a slightly sweeter flavor.
- Customize your salad by adding cherry tomatoes, bell peppers, or olives for extra color and texture.
- This salad is best served fresh but can be stored in the refrigerator in an airtight container for up to 2 days.

Cucumber Salad with Yogurt Dressing is a perfect dish for hot summer days, providing a cool and creamy complement to any meal. Enjoy the crispness of the cucumbers and the tangy richness of the yogurt dressing in every bite!

Broccoli Salad with Cranberries and Sunflower Seeds

Ingredients:

For the Salad:

- 4 cups broccoli florets, cut into bite-sized pieces
- 1/2 cup dried cranberries
- 1/4 cup red onion, finely chopped
- 1/4 cup sunflower seeds, toasted
- Optional: 1/4 cup crumbled bacon or vegetarian bacon bits
- Optional: 1/4 cup crumbled feta cheese or shredded cheddar cheese

For the Dressing:

- 1/2 cup mayonnaise (you can use reduced-fat or vegan mayo)
- 2 tablespoons apple cider vinegar or white vinegar
- 1 tablespoon honey or maple syrup
- Salt and freshly ground black pepper, to taste

Instructions:

1. **Prepare the Broccoli:**
    - Cut the broccoli florets into bite-sized pieces. You can blanch them in boiling water for 1-2 minutes for a more tender texture, then drain and rinse under cold water to stop the cooking process. Alternatively, you can use them raw for added crunch.
2. **Make the Dressing:**
    - In a small bowl, whisk together the mayonnaise, apple cider vinegar, honey or maple syrup, salt, and pepper until smooth and well combined.
3. **Assemble the Salad:**
    - In a large salad bowl, combine the broccoli florets, dried cranberries, finely chopped red onion, toasted sunflower seeds, and optional crumbled bacon or vegetarian bacon bits.
4. **Add Dressing:**
    - Pour the dressing over the broccoli salad ingredients.
5. **Toss Gently:**
    - Gently toss all the ingredients together until the broccoli and other ingredients are evenly coated with the dressing.
6. **Add Optional Cheese:**

- If using, sprinkle crumbled feta cheese or shredded cheddar cheese over the salad.
7. **Chill (Optional):**
    - For best flavor, refrigerate the Broccoli Salad with Cranberries and Sunflower Seeds for at least 30 minutes before serving to allow the flavors to meld together.
8. **Serve:**
    - Serve the Broccoli Salad chilled or at room temperature as a delicious side dish or a light meal.

Tips:

- Customize the salad by adding sliced almonds or pecans instead of sunflower seeds.
- Add a squeeze of fresh lemon juice or zest for a hint of citrus flavor.
- This salad can be made ahead of time and stored in the refrigerator in an airtight container for up to 3 days.

Broccoli Salad with Cranberries and Sunflower Seeds is a versatile and colorful dish that's perfect for picnics, barbecues, or as a healthy addition to any meal. Enjoy the combination of crunchy broccoli, sweet cranberries, and nutty sunflower seeds in every bite!

Edamame Salad

Ingredients:

For the Salad:

- 2 cups shelled edamame beans (fresh or frozen, thawed)
- 1 red bell pepper, diced
- 1 cup cherry tomatoes, halved
- 1/2 cucumber, diced
- 1/4 cup red onion, finely chopped
- 1/4 cup fresh cilantro or parsley, chopped
- Optional: 1/4 cup crumbled feta cheese or diced avocado

For the Dressing:

- 3 tablespoons rice vinegar or apple cider vinegar
- 2 tablespoons soy sauce or tamari (for gluten-free option)
- 1 tablespoon sesame oil
- 1 tablespoon honey or maple syrup
- 1 clove garlic, minced
- 1 teaspoon grated fresh ginger
- Salt and freshly ground black pepper, to taste

Instructions:

1. **Prepare the Edamame:**
    - If using frozen edamame, thaw them according to package instructions. If using fresh edamame, blanch them in boiling water for 3-4 minutes until tender, then drain and rinse under cold water to stop the cooking process.
2. **Make the Dressing:**
    - In a small bowl, whisk together the rice vinegar or apple cider vinegar, soy sauce or tamari, sesame oil, honey or maple syrup, minced garlic, grated ginger, salt, and pepper until well combined.
3. **Assemble the Salad:**
    - In a large salad bowl, combine the cooked and cooled edamame beans, diced red bell pepper, halved cherry tomatoes, diced cucumber, finely chopped red onion, and chopped fresh cilantro or parsley.
4. **Add Dressing:**
    - Pour the dressing over the salad ingredients.
5. **Toss Gently:**

       - Gently toss all the ingredients together until the edamame and vegetables are evenly coated with the dressing.
6. **Add Optional Ingredients:**
       - If using, sprinkle crumbled feta cheese or diced avocado over the salad.
7. **Chill (Optional):**
       - For best flavor, refrigerate the Edamame Salad for at least 30 minutes before serving to allow the flavors to meld together.
8. **Serve:**
       - Serve the Edamame Salad chilled or at room temperature as a nutritious and satisfying side dish or light meal.

Tips:

- You can add other vegetables such as shredded carrots, diced bell peppers, or sliced radishes for extra crunch and color.
- Customize the dressing by adjusting the sweetness or adding more soy sauce for a saltier flavor.
- This salad can be stored in the refrigerator in an airtight container for up to 3 days.

Edamame Salad is a healthy and protein-packed dish that's perfect for picnics, potlucks, or as a refreshing addition to any meal. Enjoy the combination of tender edamame beans, crisp vegetables, and flavorful dressing in every bite!

Mango Avocado Salad

Ingredients:

For the Salad:

- 2 ripe mangoes, peeled, pitted, and diced
- 2 ripe avocados, peeled, pitted, and diced
- 1/4 cup red onion, thinly sliced
- 1/4 cup fresh cilantro, chopped
- Optional: 1/4 cup cherry tomatoes, halved
- Optional: 1/4 cup crumbled feta cheese or diced mozzarella balls (bocconcini)

For the Dressing:

- 2 tablespoons lime juice (about 1-2 limes)
- 2 tablespoons extra virgin olive oil
- 1 tablespoon honey or maple syrup
- 1 teaspoon Dijon mustard
- Salt and freshly ground black pepper, to taste

Instructions:

1. **Prepare the Salad:**
    - In a large salad bowl, combine the diced mangoes, diced avocados, thinly sliced red onion, chopped fresh cilantro, and optional cherry tomatoes.
2. **Make the Dressing:**
    - In a small bowl, whisk together the lime juice, extra virgin olive oil, honey or maple syrup, Dijon mustard, salt, and pepper until well combined.
3. **Assemble the Salad:**
    - Pour the dressing over the mango and avocado mixture.
4. **Toss Gently:**
    - Gently toss all the ingredients together until the mangoes, avocados, and other ingredients are evenly coated with the dressing.
5. **Add Optional Ingredients:**
    - If using, sprinkle crumbled feta cheese or diced mozzarella balls over the salad.
6. **Chill (Optional):**
    - For best flavor, refrigerate the Mango Avocado Salad for at least 30 minutes before serving to allow the flavors to meld together.
7. **Serve:**

- Serve the Mango Avocado Salad chilled or at room temperature as a refreshing and nutritious side dish or a light meal.

Tips:

- Choose ripe but firm mangoes and avocados for the best texture and flavor.
- Adjust the sweetness and acidity of the dressing to your taste preferences by varying the amount of honey or lime juice.
- Garnish with additional cilantro leaves or a sprinkle of chili flakes for added flavor and color.
- This salad is best served fresh but can be stored in the refrigerator in an airtight container for up to 1 day.

Mango Avocado Salad is a colorful and flavorful dish that's perfect for summer gatherings or as a vibrant addition to any meal. Enjoy the creamy avocado, sweet mango, and zesty dressing in every bite!

Radicchio and Orange Salad

Ingredients:

For the Salad:

- 1 head of radicchio, thinly sliced
- 2 oranges, peeled and sliced into rounds or segments
- 1/4 cup red onion, thinly sliced
- 1/4 cup toasted walnuts or pecans, chopped
- Optional: 1/4 cup crumbled goat cheese or feta cheese

For the Dressing:

- 3 tablespoons extra virgin olive oil
- 2 tablespoons balsamic vinegar
- 1 tablespoon honey or maple syrup
- 1 teaspoon Dijon mustard
- Salt and freshly ground black pepper, to taste

Instructions:

1. **Prepare the Salad:**
    - In a large salad bowl, combine the thinly sliced radicchio, orange slices or segments, thinly sliced red onion, and toasted chopped nuts.
2. **Make the Dressing:**
    - In a small bowl, whisk together the extra virgin olive oil, balsamic vinegar, honey or maple syrup, Dijon mustard, salt, and pepper until well combined.
3. **Assemble the Salad:**
    - Pour the dressing over the radicchio and orange mixture.
4. **Toss Gently:**
    - Gently toss all the ingredients together until the radicchio, oranges, and other ingredients are evenly coated with the dressing.
5. **Add Optional Ingredients:**
    - If using, sprinkle crumbled goat cheese or feta cheese over the salad.
6. **Chill (Optional):**
    - For best flavor, refrigerate the Radicchio and Orange Salad for at least 15-30 minutes before serving to allow the flavors to meld together.
7. **Serve:**
    - Serve the Radicchio and Orange Salad chilled or at room temperature as a refreshing and colorful side dish or a light meal.

Tips:

- Choose oranges that are juicy and sweet for the best flavor contrast with the bitter radicchio.
- Toasting the nuts adds extra crunch and enhances their flavor. Toast them in a dry skillet over medium heat for a few minutes until lightly browned and fragrant.
- Adjust the sweetness and acidity of the dressing to your taste by varying the amount of honey or vinegar.
- This salad is best served fresh but can be stored in the refrigerator in an airtight container for up to 1 day.

Radicchio and Orange Salad is a delightful blend of flavors and textures, making it a perfect dish for special occasions or as an elegant addition to any meal. Enjoy the unique combination of bitter radicchio, sweet oranges, and savory dressing in every bite!

Spinach and Artichoke Salad

Ingredients:

For the Salad:

- 6 cups fresh spinach leaves, washed and dried
- 1 can (14 oz) artichoke hearts, drained and quartered
- 1/2 cup cherry tomatoes, halved
- 1/4 cup red onion, thinly sliced
- 1/4 cup toasted pine nuts or almonds
- Optional: 1/4 cup grated Parmesan cheese or crumbled feta cheese

For the Dressing:

- 1/3 cup mayonnaise (you can use reduced-fat or vegan mayo)
- 1/4 cup plain Greek yogurt (or sour cream)
- 2 tablespoons lemon juice
- 1 clove garlic, minced
- 1 tablespoon Dijon mustard
- Salt and freshly ground black pepper, to taste

Instructions:

1. **Prepare the Salad:**
   - In a large salad bowl, combine the fresh spinach leaves, quartered artichoke hearts, halved cherry tomatoes, thinly sliced red onion, and toasted pine nuts or almonds.
2. **Make the Dressing:**
   - In a small bowl, whisk together the mayonnaise, Greek yogurt (or sour cream), lemon juice, minced garlic, Dijon mustard, salt, and pepper until smooth and well combined.
3. **Assemble the Salad:**
   - Pour the dressing over the spinach and artichoke mixture.
4. **Toss Gently:**
   - Gently toss all the ingredients together until the spinach, artichoke, and other ingredients are evenly coated with the dressing.
5. **Add Optional Ingredients:**
   - If using, sprinkle grated Parmesan cheese or crumbled feta cheese over the salad.
6. **Serve:**

- Serve the Spinach and Artichoke Salad chilled or at room temperature as a delicious and satisfying side dish or a light meal.

Tips:

- Adjust the creaminess of the dressing by varying the amount of mayonnaise or Greek yogurt.
- Add a pinch of dried herbs such as oregano or basil to the dressing for extra flavor.
- This salad can be made ahead of time and stored in the refrigerator in an airtight container for up to 1 day.

Spinach and Artichoke Salad is a versatile and nutritious dish that's perfect for gatherings or as a flavorful addition to any meal. Enjoy the combination of fresh spinach, tender artichoke hearts, and creamy dressing in every bite!

Israeli Salad

Ingredients:

- 2 large tomatoes, finely diced
- 1 cucumber, finely diced
- 1 red bell pepper, finely diced
- 1 green bell pepper, finely diced
- 1/2 red onion, finely diced
- 1/4 cup fresh parsley, chopped
- 1/4 cup fresh mint, chopped (optional)
- Juice of 1-2 lemons (about 4 tablespoons)
- 3 tablespoons extra virgin olive oil
- Salt and freshly ground black pepper, to taste

Instructions:

1. **Prepare the Vegetables:**
    - Finely dice the tomatoes, cucumber, red bell pepper, green bell pepper, and red onion. You want all the vegetables to be roughly the same size for even distribution of flavors.
2. **Combine the Salad:**
    - In a large salad bowl, combine the diced tomatoes, cucumber, red and green bell peppers, and red onion.
3. **Add Herbs:**
    - Add the chopped parsley and optional chopped mint to the bowl with the vegetables.
4. **Make the Dressing:**
    - In a small bowl, whisk together the lemon juice, extra virgin olive oil, salt, and pepper until well combined.
5. **Toss the Salad:**
    - Pour the dressing over the salad ingredients.
6. **Mix Well:**
    - Gently toss all the ingredients together until the vegetables and herbs are evenly coated with the dressing.
7. **Chill (Optional):**
    - For best flavor, refrigerate the Israeli Salad for at least 15-30 minutes before serving to allow the flavors to meld together.
8. **Serve:**

- Serve the Israeli Salad chilled or at room temperature as a refreshing side dish or a light meal.

Tips:

- Customize your Israeli Salad by adding chopped olives, diced avocado, or crumbled feta cheese.
- Adjust the amount of lemon juice and olive oil to your taste preferences for a tangier or milder dressing.
- Israeli Salad is traditionally served fresh but can be stored in the refrigerator in an airtight container for up to 1 day.

Israeli Salad is a versatile and healthy dish that's perfect for picnics, barbecues, or as a refreshing addition to any meal. Enjoy the crispness of the vegetables and the zesty dressing in every bite!

Brussels Sprouts Salad with Maple Dijon Dressing

Ingredients:

For the Salad:

- 1 lb Brussels sprouts, trimmed and thinly sliced (about 4 cups)
- 1/2 cup dried cranberries or cherries
- 1/4 cup toasted pecans or walnuts, chopped
- 1/4 cup shaved Parmesan cheese or crumbled feta cheese
- Optional: 1/4 cup cooked quinoa or farro for added texture

For the Maple Dijon Dressing:

- 1/4 cup extra virgin olive oil
- 2 tablespoons apple cider vinegar or white wine vinegar
- 1 tablespoon Dijon mustard
- 1 tablespoon maple syrup
- 1 clove garlic, minced (optional)
- Salt and freshly ground black pepper, to taste

Instructions:

1. **Prepare the Brussels Sprouts:**
   - Trim the Brussels sprouts and remove any tough outer leaves. Slice them thinly using a sharp knife or a mandoline slicer. Place the sliced Brussels sprouts in a large salad bowl.
2. **Make the Dressing:**
   - In a small bowl, whisk together the extra virgin olive oil, apple cider vinegar or white wine vinegar, Dijon mustard, maple syrup, minced garlic (if using), salt, and pepper until well combined.
3. **Assemble the Salad:**
   - Add the dried cranberries or cherries, toasted chopped pecans or walnuts, and shaved Parmesan or crumbled feta cheese to the sliced Brussels sprouts.
4. **Add Optional Ingredients:**
   - If using, add the cooked quinoa or farro to the salad bowl.
5. **Pour Dressing Over Salad:**
   - Pour the Maple Dijon Dressing over the Brussels sprouts and other salad ingredients.
6. **Toss Gently:**

- Gently toss all the ingredients together until the Brussels sprouts and other ingredients are evenly coated with the dressing.
7. **Chill (Optional):**
   - For best flavor, refrigerate the Brussels Sprouts Salad with Maple Dijon Dressing for at least 15-30 minutes before serving to allow the flavors to meld together.
8. **Serve:**
   - Serve the Brussels Sprouts Salad chilled or at room temperature as a hearty and flavorful side dish or a light meal.

Tips:

- Massaging the thinly sliced Brussels sprouts with a bit of olive oil and salt before adding other ingredients can help to soften their texture and reduce bitterness.
- Adjust the sweetness and tanginess of the dressing by varying the amount of maple syrup or vinegar to suit your taste preferences.
- This salad can be stored in the refrigerator in an airtight container for up to 2 days, although it's best enjoyed fresh.

Brussels Sprouts Salad with Maple Dijon Dressing is a nutritious and satisfying dish that's perfect for fall and winter gatherings or as a flavorful addition to any meal. Enjoy the crunchy Brussels sprouts, sweet cranberries, and nutty pecans in every bite!

Roasted Eggplant Salad

Ingredients:

For the Salad:

- 2 medium eggplants, diced into 1-inch cubes
- 1 pint cherry tomatoes, halved
- 1/4 cup red onion, thinly sliced
- 1/4 cup fresh parsley, chopped
- 1/4 cup fresh basil, chopped
- 1/4 cup crumbled feta cheese or goat cheese (optional)
- 1/4 cup toasted pine nuts or chopped almonds (optional)

For the Dressing:

- 1/4 cup extra virgin olive oil
- 2 tablespoons balsamic vinegar or red wine vinegar
- 1 clove garlic, minced
- 1 teaspoon Dijon mustard
- Salt and freshly ground black pepper, to taste

Instructions:

1. **Roast the Eggplant:**
    - Preheat the oven to 400°F (200°C). Place the diced eggplant on a baking sheet lined with parchment paper. Drizzle with olive oil, season with salt and pepper, and toss to coat. Roast in the preheated oven for 25-30 minutes, or until tender and golden brown, flipping halfway through. Remove from the oven and let cool slightly.
2. **Prepare the Dressing:**
    - In a small bowl, whisk together the extra virgin olive oil, balsamic vinegar or red wine vinegar, minced garlic, Dijon mustard, salt, and pepper until well combined.
3. **Assemble the Salad:**
    - In a large salad bowl, combine the roasted eggplant cubes, halved cherry tomatoes, thinly sliced red onion, chopped fresh parsley, and chopped fresh basil.
4. **Add Optional Ingredients:**
    - If using, sprinkle crumbled feta cheese or goat cheese and toasted pine nuts or chopped almonds over the salad.

5. **Pour Dressing Over Salad:**
   - Drizzle the dressing over the eggplant and other salad ingredients.
6. **Toss Gently:**
   - Gently toss all the ingredients together until the roasted eggplant and other ingredients are evenly coated with the dressing.
7. **Chill (Optional):**
   - For best flavor, refrigerate the Roasted Eggplant Salad for at least 30 minutes before serving to allow the flavors to meld together.
8. **Serve:**
   - Serve the Roasted Eggplant Salad chilled or at room temperature as a delicious and satisfying side dish or a light meal.

Tips:

- You can customize this salad by adding olives, roasted bell peppers, or sun-dried tomatoes for additional flavor.
- Adjust the amount of garlic and vinegar in the dressing to suit your taste preferences.
- This salad can be stored in the refrigerator in an airtight container for up to 3 days.

Roasted Eggplant Salad is a versatile and nutritious dish that's perfect for any occasion, offering a delightful blend of textures and flavors. Enjoy the tender roasted eggplant paired with the freshness of tomatoes and herbs in every bite!

Black Bean and Corn Salad

Ingredients:

For the Salad:

- 2 cups cooked black beans (about 1 can, drained and rinsed)
- 2 cups corn kernels (fresh, canned, or thawed if frozen)
- 1 red bell pepper, diced
- 1/2 red onion, finely chopped
- 1 jalapeño pepper, seeded and finely chopped (optional)
- 1/4 cup fresh cilantro, chopped
- 1 avocado, diced (optional)
- Optional: 1/4 cup crumbled feta cheese or cotija cheese

For the Dressing:

- 3 tablespoons lime juice (about 2 limes)
- 3 tablespoons extra virgin olive oil
- 1 clove garlic, minced
- 1 teaspoon ground cumin
- 1/2 teaspoon chili powder (adjust to taste)
- Salt and freshly ground black pepper, to taste

Instructions:

1. **Prepare the Salad:**
    - In a large salad bowl, combine the cooked black beans, corn kernels, diced red bell pepper, finely chopped red onion, chopped jalapeño pepper (if using), and chopped fresh cilantro.
2. **Make the Dressing:**
    - In a small bowl, whisk together the lime juice, extra virgin olive oil, minced garlic, ground cumin, chili powder, salt, and pepper until well combined.
3. **Assemble the Salad:**
    - Pour the dressing over the black bean and corn mixture.
4. **Toss Gently:**
    - Gently toss all the ingredients together until the black beans, corn, and other ingredients are evenly coated with the dressing.
5. **Add Optional Ingredients:**
    - If using, gently fold in diced avocado and crumbled feta cheese or cotija cheese.

6. **Chill (Optional):**
    - For best flavor, refrigerate the Black Bean and Corn Salad for at least 30 minutes before serving to allow the flavors to meld together.
7. **Serve:**
    - Serve the Black Bean and Corn Salad chilled or at room temperature as a delicious and nutritious side dish or a light meal.

Tips:

- Adjust the amount of chili powder and jalapeño pepper to your desired level of spiciness.
- Customize the salad by adding diced tomatoes, chopped green onions, or a squeeze of fresh orange juice for a hint of sweetness.
- This salad can be stored in the refrigerator in an airtight container for up to 3 days.

Black Bean and Corn Salad is a versatile dish that's perfect for picnics, barbecues, or as a healthy addition to any meal. Enjoy the combination of hearty black beans, sweet corn, and zesty dressing in every bite!

Tabbouleh Salad

Ingredients:

For the Salad:

- 1 cup bulgur wheat
- 1 1/2 cups boiling water
- 1 1/2 cups fresh parsley, finely chopped
- 1/2 cup fresh mint leaves, finely chopped
- 4-5 green onions, finely chopped
- 1 cucumber, seeded and finely diced
- 2 medium tomatoes, seeded and finely diced
- 1/4 cup lemon juice (about 2 lemons)
- 1/4 cup extra virgin olive oil
- Salt and freshly ground black pepper, to taste

Instructions:

1. **Prepare the Bulgur Wheat:**
   - Place the bulgur wheat in a heatproof bowl. Pour boiling water over the bulgur wheat, cover with a lid or plate, and let it sit for about 20-30 minutes, or until the bulgur is tender and has absorbed all the water. Fluff with a fork and let it cool to room temperature.
2. **Chop the Herbs and Vegetables:**
   - While the bulgur wheat is soaking, finely chop the fresh parsley and mint leaves. Finely dice the green onions, cucumber, and tomatoes.
3. **Assemble the Salad:**
   - In a large salad bowl, combine the cooled bulgur wheat, chopped parsley, chopped mint, diced green onions, diced cucumber, and diced tomatoes.
4. **Make the Dressing:**
   - In a small bowl, whisk together the lemon juice and extra virgin olive oil. Season with salt and pepper to taste.
5. **Combine and Toss:**
   - Pour the dressing over the salad ingredients.
6. **Mix Well:**
   - Gently toss all the ingredients together until the bulgur wheat, herbs, vegetables, and dressing are evenly combined.
7. **Chill (Optional):**

- For best flavor, refrigerate the Tabbouleh Salad for at least 1 hour before serving to allow the flavors to meld together.
8. **Serve:**
    - Serve the Tabbouleh Salad chilled or at room temperature as a refreshing side dish or a light meal.

Tips:

- Adjust the amount of lemon juice and olive oil in the dressing according to your taste preferences.
- Tabbouleh Salad is traditionally served fresh but can be stored in the refrigerator in an airtight container for up to 2 days.
- For added flavor and texture, you can sprinkle some crumbled feta cheese or diced avocado over the salad before serving.

Tabbouleh Salad is a classic dish that's perfect for summer gatherings or as a vibrant addition to any Mediterranean-inspired meal. Enjoy the fresh herbs, crisp vegetables, and tangy dressing in every bite!

Spinach Salad with Strawberries and Walnuts

Ingredients:

For the Salad:

- 6 cups fresh spinach leaves, washed and dried
- 1 cup strawberries, hulled and sliced
- 1/2 cup walnuts, toasted and chopped
- 1/4 cup red onion, thinly sliced
- 1/4 cup crumbled feta cheese or goat cheese (optional)

For the Dressing:

- 1/4 cup extra virgin olive oil
- 2 tablespoons balsamic vinegar
- 1 tablespoon honey or maple syrup
- 1 teaspoon Dijon mustard
- Salt and freshly ground black pepper, to taste

Instructions:

1. **Prepare the Salad:**
    - In a large salad bowl, combine the fresh spinach leaves, sliced strawberries, toasted and chopped walnuts, thinly sliced red onion, and crumbled feta or goat cheese (if using).
2. **Make the Dressing:**
    - In a small bowl, whisk together the extra virgin olive oil, balsamic vinegar, honey or maple syrup, Dijon mustard, salt, and pepper until well combined.
3. **Assemble the Salad:**
    - Drizzle the dressing over the spinach, strawberries, and walnut mixture.
4. **Toss Gently:**
    - Gently toss all the ingredients together until the spinach, strawberries, walnuts, and other ingredients are evenly coated with the dressing.
5. **Serve:**
    - Serve the Spinach Salad with Strawberries and Walnuts immediately as a refreshing and flavorful side dish or a light meal.

Tips:

- For a variation, you can use mixed greens instead of spinach or add other berries like blueberries or raspberries.
- Adjust the sweetness and acidity of the dressing by varying the amount of honey or vinegar to suit your taste preferences.
- This salad is best enjoyed fresh but can be stored in the refrigerator in an airtight container for up to 1 day.

Spinach Salad with Strawberries and Walnuts is a perfect combination of textures and flavors, making it ideal for spring and summer gatherings or as a nutritious addition to any meal. Enjoy the crisp spinach, sweet strawberries, crunchy walnuts, and tangy dressing in every bite!

Fennel and Orange Salad

Ingredients:

For the Salad:

- 2 fennel bulbs, thinly sliced (reserve some fronds for garnish)
- 2 oranges, peeled and sliced into rounds or segments
- 1/4 cup red onion, thinly sliced
- 1/4 cup pitted Kalamata olives, sliced (optional)
- 1/4 cup fresh parsley leaves, chopped (optional)
- 1/4 cup toasted pine nuts or slivered almonds (optional)

For the Dressing:

- 1/4 cup extra virgin olive oil
- 2 tablespoons white wine vinegar or lemon juice
- 1 teaspoon Dijon mustard
- 1 teaspoon honey or maple syrup
- Salt and freshly ground black pepper, to taste

Instructions:

1. **Prepare the Fennel and Oranges:**
   - Trim the fennel bulbs, remove the tough outer layer, and thinly slice them. Peel the oranges and slice them into rounds or segments.
2. **Assemble the Salad:**
   - In a large salad bowl, combine the sliced fennel bulbs, orange slices, thinly sliced red onion, and optional sliced Kalamata olives, chopped parsley leaves, and toasted pine nuts or slivered almonds.
3. **Make the Dressing:**
   - In a small bowl, whisk together the extra virgin olive oil, white wine vinegar or lemon juice, Dijon mustard, honey or maple syrup, salt, and pepper until well combined.
4. **Pour Dressing Over Salad:**
   - Drizzle the dressing over the fennel, oranges, and other salad ingredients.
5. **Toss Gently:**
   - Gently toss all the ingredients together until the fennel, oranges, and other ingredients are evenly coated with the dressing.
6. **Chill (Optional):**

- For best flavor, refrigerate the Fennel and Orange Salad for at least 15-30 minutes before serving to allow the flavors to meld together.
7. **Serve:**
    - Garnish with reserved fennel fronds and serve the Fennel and Orange Salad chilled or at room temperature as a refreshing and vibrant side dish or a light meal.

Tips:

- Adjust the sweetness and acidity of the dressing by varying the amount of honey or vinegar to suit your taste preferences.
- This salad can be stored in the refrigerator in an airtight container for up to 1 day, although it's best enjoyed fresh.

Fennel and Orange Salad is a wonderful combination of flavors and textures, perfect for any occasion, offering a delightful blend of crisp fennel, juicy oranges, and tangy dressing in every bite!

Thai Noodle Salad

Ingredients:

For the Salad:

- 8 oz (225g) rice noodles (thin or medium), cooked according to package instructions and cooled
- 1 red bell pepper, thinly sliced
- 1 carrot, julienned or grated
- 1 cucumber, thinly sliced or julienned
- 1 cup shredded cabbage or coleslaw mix
- 1/2 cup fresh cilantro leaves, chopped
- 1/4 cup fresh mint leaves, chopped
- 1/4 cup roasted peanuts, chopped (optional)
- Optional: 1/2 cup cooked and shredded chicken, tofu, or shrimp

For the Dressing:

- 1/4 cup lime juice (about 2 limes)
- 3 tablespoons soy sauce (or tamari for gluten-free)
- 2 tablespoons sesame oil
- 2 tablespoons honey or maple syrup
- 1 tablespoon fresh ginger, grated
- 1 clove garlic, minced
- 1 tablespoon sriracha or chili garlic sauce (adjust to taste)

Instructions:

1. **Prepare the Dressing:**
    - In a small bowl, whisk together the lime juice, soy sauce, sesame oil, honey or maple syrup, grated ginger, minced garlic, and sriracha or chili garlic sauce until well combined. Set aside.
2. **Assemble the Salad:**
    - In a large mixing bowl, combine the cooked and cooled rice noodles with the sliced red bell pepper, julienned carrot, sliced cucumber, shredded cabbage or coleslaw mix, chopped cilantro, chopped mint, and roasted peanuts (if using).
3. **Add Protein (Optional):**
    - If desired, add cooked and shredded chicken, tofu, or shrimp to the salad ingredients.

4. **Pour Dressing Over Salad:**
   - Drizzle the prepared dressing over the salad ingredients.
5. **Toss Gently:**
   - Gently toss all the ingredients together until the noodles and vegetables are evenly coated with the dressing.
6. **Chill (Optional):**
   - For best flavor, refrigerate the Thai Noodle Salad for at least 30 minutes before serving to allow the flavors to meld together.
7. **Serve:**
   - Serve the Thai Noodle Salad chilled or at room temperature as a refreshing and satisfying main dish or side dish.

Tips:

- Customize the salad by adding other vegetables like bean sprouts, snap peas, or bell peppers.
- Adjust the spiciness of the dressing by varying the amount of sriracha or chili garlic sauce.
- Garnish with additional chopped peanuts, cilantro leaves, or lime wedges before serving for extra flavor and presentation.

Thai Noodle Salad is a versatile and delicious dish that's perfect for lunch, dinner, or as a vibrant addition to a potluck or picnic. Enjoy the blend of tangy, sweet, and spicy flavors with every forkful!

Roasted Vegetable Salad

Ingredients:

For the Salad:

- 2 fennel bulbs, thinly sliced (reserve some fronds for garnish)
- 2 oranges, peeled and sliced into rounds or segments
- 1/4 cup red onion, thinly sliced
- 1/4 cup pitted Kalamata olives, sliced (optional)
- 1/4 cup fresh parsley leaves, chopped (optional)
- 1/4 cup toasted pine nuts or slivered almonds (optional)

For the Dressing:

- 1/4 cup extra virgin olive oil
- 2 tablespoons white wine vinegar or lemon juice
- 1 teaspoon Dijon mustard
- 1 teaspoon honey or maple syrup
- Salt and freshly ground black pepper, to taste

Instructions:

1. **Prepare the Fennel and Oranges:**
    - Trim the fennel bulbs, remove the tough outer layer, and thinly slice them. Peel the oranges and slice them into rounds or segments.
2. **Assemble the Salad:**
    - In a large salad bowl, combine the sliced fennel bulbs, orange slices, thinly sliced red onion, and optional sliced Kalamata olives, chopped parsley leaves, and toasted pine nuts or slivered almonds.
3. **Make the Dressing:**
    - In a small bowl, whisk together the extra virgin olive oil, white wine vinegar or lemon juice, Dijon mustard, honey or maple syrup, salt, and pepper until well combined.
4. **Pour Dressing Over Salad:**
    - Drizzle the dressing over the fennel, oranges, and other salad ingredients.
5. **Toss Gently:**
    - Gently toss all the ingredients together until the fennel, oranges, and other ingredients are evenly coated with the dressing.
6. **Chill (Optional):**

- For best flavor, refrigerate the Fennel and Orange Salad for at least 15-30 minutes before serving to allow the flavors to meld together.
7. **Serve:**
    - Garnish with reserved fennel fronds and serve the Fennel and Orange Salad chilled or at room temperature as a refreshing and vibrant side dish or a light meal.

Tips:

- Adjust the sweetness and acidity of the dressing by varying the amount of honey or vinegar to suit your taste preferences.
- This salad can be stored in the refrigerator in an airtight container for up to 1 day, although it's best enjoyed fresh.

Fennel and Orange Salad is a wonderful combination of flavors and textures, perfect for any occasion, offering a delightful blend of crisp fennel, juicy oranges, and tangy dressing in every bite!

Thai Noodle Salad

Ingredients:

For the Salad:

- 8 oz (225g) rice noodles (thin or medium), cooked according to package instructions and cooled
- 1 red bell pepper, thinly sliced
- 1 carrot, julienned or grated
- 1 cucumber, thinly sliced or julienned
- 1 cup shredded cabbage or coleslaw mix
- 1/2 cup fresh cilantro leaves, chopped
- 1/4 cup fresh mint leaves, chopped
- 1/4 cup roasted peanuts, chopped (optional)
- Optional: 1/2 cup cooked and shredded chicken, tofu, or shrimp

For the Dressing:

- 1/4 cup lime juice (about 2 limes)
- 3 tablespoons soy sauce (or tamari for gluten-free)
- 2 tablespoons sesame oil
- 2 tablespoons honey or maple syrup
- 1 tablespoon fresh ginger, grated
- 1 clove garlic, minced
- 1 tablespoon sriracha or chili garlic sauce (adjust to taste)

Instructions:

1. **Prepare the Dressing:**
   - In a small bowl, whisk together the lime juice, soy sauce, sesame oil, honey or maple syrup, grated ginger, minced garlic, and sriracha or chili garlic sauce until well combined. Set aside.
2. **Assemble the Salad:**
   - In a large mixing bowl, combine the cooked and cooled rice noodles with the sliced red bell pepper, julienned carrot, sliced cucumber, shredded cabbage or coleslaw mix, chopped cilantro, chopped mint, and roasted peanuts (if using).
3. **Add Protein (Optional):**
   - If desired, add cooked and shredded chicken, tofu, or shrimp to the salad ingredients.

4. **Pour Dressing Over Salad:**
   - Drizzle the prepared dressing over the salad ingredients.
5. **Toss Gently:**
   - Gently toss all the ingredients together until the noodles and vegetables are evenly coated with the dressing.
6. **Chill (Optional):**
   - For best flavor, refrigerate the Thai Noodle Salad for at least 30 minutes before serving to allow the flavors to meld together.
7. **Serve:**
   - Serve the Thai Noodle Salad chilled or at room temperature as a refreshing and satisfying main dish or side dish.

Tips:

- Customize the salad by adding other vegetables like bean sprouts, snap peas, or bell peppers.
- Adjust the spiciness of the dressing by varying the amount of sriracha or chili garlic sauce.
- Garnish with additional chopped peanuts, cilantro leaves, or lime wedges before serving for extra flavor and presentation.

Thai Noodle Salad is a versatile and delicious dish that's perfect for lunch, dinner, or as a vibrant addition to a potluck or picnic. Enjoy the blend of tangy, sweet, and spicy flavors with every forkful!

Roasted Vegetable Salad

Ingredients:

For the Salad:

- 2 cups cherry tomatoes, halved
- 1 red bell pepper, cut into strips
- 1 yellow bell pepper, cut into strips
- 1 zucchini, sliced into rounds
- 1 yellow squash, sliced into rounds
- 1 red onion, cut into wedges
- 1 cup baby spinach leaves
- 1/4 cup fresh basil leaves, torn
- 1/4 cup crumbled feta cheese or goat cheese (optional)
- 1/4 cup toasted pine nuts or chopped almonds (optional)

For the Dressing:

- 1/4 cup extra virgin olive oil
- 2 tablespoons balsamic vinegar
- 1 clove garlic, minced
- 1 teaspoon Dijon mustard
- 1 teaspoon honey or maple syrup
- Salt and freshly ground black pepper, to taste

Instructions:

1. **Prepare the Roasted Vegetables:**
   - Preheat the oven to 400°F (200°C). Place the cherry tomatoes, red bell pepper, yellow bell pepper, zucchini, yellow squash, and red onion on a large baking sheet. Drizzle with olive oil, season with salt and pepper, and toss to coat evenly. Spread the vegetables out in a single layer.
2. **Roast the Vegetables:**
   - Roast in the preheated oven for 20-25 minutes, or until the vegetables are tender and slightly caramelized, stirring halfway through cooking. Remove from the oven and let cool slightly.
3. **Make the Dressing:**
   - In a small bowl, whisk together the extra virgin olive oil, balsamic vinegar, minced garlic, Dijon mustard, honey or maple syrup, salt, and pepper until well combined.

4. **Assemble the Salad:**
   - In a large salad bowl, combine the roasted vegetables with the baby spinach leaves and torn basil leaves.
5. **Add Optional Ingredients:**
   - If using, sprinkle crumbled feta cheese or goat cheese and toasted pine nuts or chopped almonds over the salad.
6. **Pour Dressing Over Salad:**
   - Drizzle the dressing over the roasted vegetables and other salad ingredients.
7. **Toss Gently:**
   - Gently toss all the ingredients together until the roasted vegetables, spinach, basil, and optional ingredients are evenly coated with the dressing.
8. **Serve:**
   - Serve the Roasted Vegetable Salad immediately as a satisfying main dish or side dish.

Tips:

- You can use any combination of your favorite vegetables for roasting, such as eggplant, mushrooms, or carrots.
- Adjust the sweetness and acidity of the dressing by varying the amount of honey or vinegar to suit your taste preferences.
- This salad can be enjoyed warm or at room temperature. Leftovers can be stored in the refrigerator in an airtight container for up to 3 days.

Roasted Vegetable Salad is a versatile and nutritious dish that's perfect for any season, offering a delicious blend of textures and flavors from the caramelized vegetables, fresh greens, and tangy dressing. Enjoy the rich and satisfying taste of roasted vegetables in every bite!

Grilled Peach Salad

Ingredients:

For the Salad:

- 4 ripe peaches, halved and pitted
- 6 cups mixed greens (such as arugula, baby spinach, or mesclun)
- 1/2 cup crumbled goat cheese or feta cheese
- 1/4 cup toasted pecans or walnuts, chopped
- 1/4 cup red onion, thinly sliced
- Optional: 1/4 cup fresh basil or mint leaves, torn

For the Dressing:

- 1/4 cup extra virgin olive oil
- 2 tablespoons balsamic vinegar
- 1 teaspoon honey or maple syrup
- Salt and freshly ground black pepper, to taste

Instructions:

1. **Grill the Peaches:**
    - Preheat the grill or grill pan over medium-high heat. Lightly brush the peach halves with olive oil. Grill the peaches cut side down for about 3-4 minutes, or until grill marks appear and the peaches are slightly softened. Flip and grill for another 2-3 minutes. Remove from heat and let cool slightly.
2. **Prepare the Dressing:**
    - In a small bowl, whisk together the extra virgin olive oil, balsamic vinegar, honey or maple syrup, salt, and pepper until well combined.
3. **Assemble the Salad:**
    - Arrange the mixed greens on a serving platter or in a large salad bowl.
4. **Slice the Peaches:**
    - Slice the grilled peach halves into wedges or chunks.
5. **Add Salad Ingredients:**
    - Scatter the sliced grilled peaches, crumbled goat cheese or feta cheese, chopped toasted pecans or walnuts, thinly sliced red onion, and torn basil or mint leaves (if using) over the mixed greens.
6. **Drizzle with Dressing:**
    - Drizzle the dressing over the salad ingredients.

7. **Toss Gently:**
   - Gently toss the Grilled Peach Salad together to combine all the ingredients and coat them with the dressing.
8. **Serve:**
   - Serve the Grilled Peach Salad immediately as a refreshing and flavorful side dish or light main course.

Tips:

- You can substitute the mixed greens with your favorite lettuce or salad greens.
- Adjust the sweetness and acidity of the dressing by varying the amount of honey or vinegar to suit your taste preferences.
- Grilled Peach Salad pairs well with grilled chicken or shrimp for added protein, making it a complete meal.

Grilled Peach Salad is a perfect dish for summer gatherings or anytime you want to enjoy the delicious combination of grilled fruit, fresh greens, and tangy dressing. Enjoy the sweet and savory flavors with every bite!

Quinoa Greek Salad

Ingredients:

For the Salad:

- 1 cup quinoa, rinsed
- 2 cups water or vegetable broth
- 1 cucumber, diced
- 1 pint cherry tomatoes, halved
- 1/2 red onion, thinly sliced
- 1/2 cup Kalamata olives, pitted and halved
- 1/2 cup crumbled feta cheese
- 1/4 cup fresh parsley, chopped
- Optional: 1/4 cup chopped fresh mint

For the Dressing:

- 1/4 cup extra virgin olive oil
- 3 tablespoons red wine vinegar
- 1 teaspoon dried oregano
- 1 clove garlic, minced
- Salt and freshly ground black pepper, to taste

Instructions:

1. **Cook the Quinoa:**
    - In a medium saucepan, combine the quinoa and water or vegetable broth. Bring to a boil, then reduce heat to low, cover, and simmer for 15-20 minutes, or until quinoa is cooked and water is absorbed. Remove from heat and let it cool.
2. **Prepare the Dressing:**
    - In a small bowl, whisk together the extra virgin olive oil, red wine vinegar, dried oregano, minced garlic, salt, and pepper until well combined. Set aside.
3. **Assemble the Salad:**
    - In a large salad bowl, combine the cooked and cooled quinoa with the diced cucumber, halved cherry tomatoes, thinly sliced red onion, halved Kalamata olives, crumbled feta cheese, chopped fresh parsley, and chopped fresh mint (if using).
4. **Add Dressing:**

        - Pour the dressing over the quinoa and vegetable mixture.
5. **Toss Gently:**
        - Gently toss all the ingredients together until the quinoa and vegetables are evenly coated with the dressing.
6. **Chill (Optional):**
        - For best flavor, refrigerate the Quinoa Greek Salad for at least 30 minutes before serving to allow the flavors to meld together.
7. **Serve:**
        - Serve the Quinoa Greek Salad chilled or at room temperature as a nutritious and flavorful side dish or light meal.

Tips:

- You can customize this salad by adding other ingredients such as diced bell peppers, artichoke hearts, or diced avocado.
- Adjust the seasoning and acidity of the dressing to your taste preferences by varying the amount of vinegar or adding a squeeze of lemon juice.
- This salad can be stored in the refrigerator in an airtight container for up to 3 days. If making ahead, add the fresh herbs just before serving to maintain their freshness.

Quinoa Greek Salad is packed with protein, fiber, and vibrant flavors, making it a perfect choice for a healthy lunch or a side dish for any occasion. Enjoy the combination of quinoa, fresh vegetables, tangy feta cheese, and Mediterranean-inspired dressing in every bite!

Cauliflower Salad with Lemon Tahini Dressing

Ingredients:

For the Salad:

- 1 head cauliflower, cut into florets
- 2 tablespoons olive oil
- Salt and freshly ground black pepper, to taste
- 1/2 cup cherry tomatoes, halved
- 1/4 cup red onion, thinly sliced
- 1/4 cup fresh parsley, chopped
- 1/4 cup toasted pine nuts or chopped almonds
- Optional: 1/4 cup crumbled feta cheese or goat cheese

For the Lemon Tahini Dressing:

- 1/4 cup tahini
- 1/4 cup water
- 3 tablespoons fresh lemon juice
- 1 clove garlic, minced
- 1 tablespoon olive oil
- 1 teaspoon honey or maple syrup
- Salt and freshly ground black pepper, to taste

Instructions:

1. **Roast the Cauliflower:**
    - Preheat the oven to 400°F (200°C). Toss the cauliflower florets with olive oil, salt, and pepper on a baking sheet. Roast for 25-30 minutes, or until cauliflower is tender and golden brown, stirring halfway through. Remove from oven and let cool slightly.
2. **Make the Lemon Tahini Dressing:**
    - In a small bowl, whisk together tahini, water, fresh lemon juice, minced garlic, olive oil, honey or maple syrup, salt, and pepper until smooth and well combined. Adjust consistency with more water if needed.
3. **Assemble the Salad:**
    - In a large salad bowl, combine the roasted cauliflower florets with cherry tomatoes, thinly sliced red onion, chopped fresh parsley, and toasted pine nuts or chopped almonds.
4. **Add Optional Ingredients:**

- If using, sprinkle crumbled feta cheese or goat cheese over the salad.
5. **Pour Dressing Over Salad:**
   - Drizzle the lemon tahini dressing over the salad ingredients.
6. **Toss Gently:**
   - Gently toss all the ingredients together until the cauliflower and other salad ingredients are evenly coated with the dressing.
7. **Serve:**
   - Serve the Cauliflower Salad with Lemon Tahini Dressing immediately as a delicious and nutritious side dish or light meal.

Tips:

- Customize the salad by adding other vegetables such as roasted bell peppers or carrots.
- Adjust the sweetness and tanginess of the dressing to your taste preferences by varying the amount of lemon juice or honey/maple syrup.
- This salad can be enjoyed warm or at room temperature. Leftovers can be stored in the refrigerator in an airtight container for up to 3 days.

Cauliflower Salad with Lemon Tahini Dressing offers a creamy texture from the tahini dressing and the nutty flavor of roasted cauliflower, complemented by fresh herbs and crunchy nuts. Enjoy the combination of flavors and textures in every bite!

Tomato Basil Mozzarella Salad

Ingredients:

- 3-4 ripe tomatoes, sliced into rounds
- 1-2 balls of fresh mozzarella cheese, sliced into rounds
- Fresh basil leaves
- Extra virgin olive oil
- Balsamic vinegar (optional)
- Salt and freshly ground black pepper, to taste

Instructions:

1. **Prepare the Ingredients:**
    - Slice the tomatoes and fresh mozzarella into rounds of equal thickness.
2. **Assemble the Salad:**
    - On a large serving platter or individual plates, alternate slices of tomato, mozzarella, and basil leaves. Arrange them in a circular pattern or overlapping layers.
3. **Drizzle with Olive Oil:**
    - Drizzle extra virgin olive oil over the tomato and mozzarella slices. Use a good quality olive oil for the best flavor.
4. **Season:**
    - Sprinkle salt and freshly ground black pepper over the salad to taste.
5. **Optional Balsamic Vinegar:**
    - For added flavor, you can drizzle a small amount of balsamic vinegar over the salad. Balsamic glaze or reduction also works well.
6. **Serve:**
    - Serve the Tomato Basil Mozzarella Salad immediately as a refreshing appetizer or side dish.

Tips:

- Use ripe and flavorful tomatoes for the best taste. Heirloom tomatoes or cherry tomatoes can add variety and color to the salad.
- Fresh mozzarella cheese (also known as mozzarella di bufala) works best for this salad due to its creamy texture and mild flavor.
- Garnish with extra basil leaves or a sprinkle of dried oregano for additional flavor.

This Tomato Basil Mozzarella Salad is a perfect choice for summer gatherings or as a light and healthy appetizer any time of the year. Enjoy the combination of fresh tomatoes, creamy mozzarella, aromatic basil, and olive oil in every bite!

Asian Cabbage Salad

Ingredients:

For the Salad:

- 4 cups shredded green cabbage
- 2 cups shredded red cabbage
- 1 large carrot, julienned or grated
- 1 red bell pepper, thinly sliced
- 1/2 cup edamame (cooked and shelled)
- 1/4 cup sliced green onions (scallions)
- 1/4 cup chopped fresh cilantro
- 1/4 cup chopped fresh mint
- 1/4 cup toasted sesame seeds (optional)
- 1/4 cup chopped peanuts or almonds (optional)

For the Dressing:

- 3 tablespoons soy sauce (or tamari for gluten-free)
- 2 tablespoons rice vinegar
- 1 tablespoon sesame oil
- 1 tablespoon honey or maple syrup
- 1 clove garlic, minced
- 1 teaspoon freshly grated ginger
- 1 teaspoon sriracha or chili garlic sauce (adjust to taste)
- Salt and pepper, to taste

Instructions:

1. **Prepare the Salad:**
   - In a large bowl, combine the shredded green cabbage, shredded red cabbage, julienned or grated carrot, thinly sliced red bell pepper, edamame, sliced green onions, chopped cilantro, and chopped mint. Toss gently to combine.
2. **Make the Dressing:**
   - In a small bowl, whisk together the soy sauce (or tamari), rice vinegar, sesame oil, honey or maple syrup, minced garlic, grated ginger, sriracha or chili garlic sauce, salt, and pepper until well combined.
3. **Assemble the Salad:**
   - Pour the dressing over the salad ingredients.

4. **Toss Gently:**
   - Gently toss all the ingredients together until the cabbage and other salad ingredients are evenly coated with the dressing.
5. **Chill (Optional):**
   - For best flavor, refrigerate the Asian Cabbage Salad for at least 30 minutes before serving to allow the flavors to meld together.
6. **Serve:**
   - Serve the Asian Cabbage Salad chilled or at room temperature as a refreshing and crunchy side dish or light meal.

Tips:

- Customize the salad by adding sliced cucumber, snap peas, or shredded radishes.
- Adjust the sweetness and spiciness of the dressing to your taste preference by varying the amount of honey/maple syrup and sriracha/chili garlic sauce.
- Garnish with toasted sesame seeds and chopped peanuts or almonds for added texture and nuttiness.

This Asian Cabbage Salad is packed with nutrients and flavor, making it a perfect dish for lunch, potlucks, or as a side to grilled meats or tofu. Enjoy the crispness of cabbage and the zesty flavors of the dressing in every bite!

Pear and Walnut Salad

Ingredients:

For the Salad:

- 6 cups mixed greens (such as baby spinach, arugula, or mesclun)
- 2 ripe pears, cored and thinly sliced
- 1/2 cup walnuts, toasted and roughly chopped
- 1/4 cup crumbled blue cheese or goat cheese (optional)
- 1/4 cup dried cranberries or pomegranate seeds (optional)

For the Dressing:

- 1/4 cup extra virgin olive oil
- 2 tablespoons balsamic vinegar
- 1 tablespoon honey or maple syrup
- 1 teaspoon Dijon mustard
- Salt and freshly ground black pepper, to taste

Instructions:

1. **Prepare the Dressing:**
    - In a small bowl, whisk together the extra virgin olive oil, balsamic vinegar, honey or maple syrup, Dijon mustard, salt, and pepper until well combined. Set aside.
2. **Assemble the Salad:**
    - In a large salad bowl, combine the mixed greens with thinly sliced pears, toasted and chopped walnuts, crumbled blue cheese or goat cheese (if using), and dried cranberries or pomegranate seeds (if using).
3. **Pour Dressing Over Salad:**
    - Drizzle the prepared dressing over the salad ingredients.
4. **Toss Gently:**
    - Gently toss all the ingredients together until the greens, pears, walnuts, and optional ingredients are evenly coated with the dressing.
5. **Serve:**
    - Serve the Pear and Walnut Salad immediately as a refreshing and flavorful side dish or light meal.

Tips:

- Adjust the sweetness and acidity of the dressing to your taste by varying the amount of honey or balsamic vinegar.
- If you prefer softer pears, you can briefly poach or grill them before adding to the salad.
- Substitute blue cheese or goat cheese with feta cheese for a different flavor profile.

This Pear and Walnut Salad is a perfect combination of textures and flavors, making it a great addition to any meal or as a standalone dish. Enjoy the sweet crunch of pears, the nuttiness of walnuts, and the tangy dressing in every bite!

Spinach and Quinoa Salad

Ingredients:

For the Salad:

- 1 cup quinoa, rinsed
- 2 cups water or vegetable broth
- 6 cups fresh baby spinach leaves
- 1 cucumber, diced
- 1 bell pepper (red, yellow, or orange), diced
- 1/2 cup cherry tomatoes, halved
- 1/4 cup red onion, thinly sliced
- 1/4 cup chopped fresh parsley or cilantro
- 1/4 cup crumbled feta cheese or goat cheese (optional)
- 1/4 cup toasted almonds or pine nuts (optional)

For the Dressing:

- 1/4 cup extra virgin olive oil
- 2 tablespoons fresh lemon juice
- 1 clove garlic, minced
- 1 teaspoon Dijon mustard
- 1 teaspoon honey or maple syrup
- Salt and freshly ground black pepper, to taste

Instructions:

1. **Cook the Quinoa:**
   - In a medium saucepan, combine the quinoa and water or vegetable broth. Bring to a boil, then reduce heat to low, cover, and simmer for 15-20 minutes, or until quinoa is cooked and liquid is absorbed. Remove from heat and let it cool.
2. **Prepare the Dressing:**
   - In a small bowl, whisk together the extra virgin olive oil, fresh lemon juice, minced garlic, Dijon mustard, honey or maple syrup, salt, and pepper until well combined.
3. **Assemble the Salad:**
   - In a large salad bowl, combine the cooked and cooled quinoa with the baby spinach leaves, diced cucumber, diced bell pepper, halved cherry tomatoes, thinly sliced red onion, and chopped fresh parsley or cilantro.

4. **Add Optional Ingredients:**
   - If using, sprinkle crumbled feta cheese or goat cheese and toasted almonds or pine nuts over the salad.
5. **Pour Dressing Over Salad:**
   - Drizzle the dressing over the salad ingredients.
6. **Toss Gently:**
   - Gently toss all the ingredients together until the quinoa, spinach, and vegetables are evenly coated with the dressing.
7. **Chill (Optional):**
   - For best flavor, refrigerate the Spinach and Quinoa Salad for at least 30 minutes before serving to allow the flavors to meld together.
8. **Serve:**
   - Serve the Spinach and Quinoa Salad chilled or at room temperature as a nutritious and satisfying side dish or light meal.

Tips:

- You can add other vegetables such as avocado, shredded carrots, or roasted sweet potatoes for added variety and nutrients.
- Adjust the sweetness and acidity of the dressing to your taste preference by varying the amount of honey or lemon juice.
- This salad can be stored in the refrigerator in an airtight container for up to 3 days. Add fresh herbs just before serving to maintain their freshness.

Enjoy the Spinach and Quinoa Salad as a wholesome and delicious way to incorporate more vegetables and whole grains into your diet!

Citrus Avocado Salad

Ingredients:

For the Salad:

- 4 cups mixed salad greens (such as baby spinach, arugula, or mixed greens)
- 2 oranges (such as navel or blood oranges), peeled and sliced
- 1 grapefruit, peeled and sliced
- 2 ripe avocados, peeled, pitted, and sliced
- 1/4 cup thinly sliced red onion
- 1/4 cup toasted sliced almonds or chopped pistachios (optional)
- Optional: 1/4 cup crumbled goat cheese or feta cheese

For the Dressing:

- 1/4 cup extra virgin olive oil
- 2 tablespoons fresh lemon juice
- 1 tablespoon fresh orange juice
- 1 teaspoon honey or maple syrup
- 1 teaspoon Dijon mustard
- Salt and freshly ground black pepper, to taste

Instructions:

1. **Prepare the Dressing:**
    - In a small bowl, whisk together the extra virgin olive oil, fresh lemon juice, fresh orange juice, honey or maple syrup, Dijon mustard, salt, and pepper until well combined. Set aside.
2. **Assemble the Salad:**
    - Arrange the mixed salad greens on a large serving platter or in a salad bowl.
3. **Layer Citrus and Avocado:**
    - Arrange the sliced oranges, grapefruit, and avocado slices over the salad greens.
4. **Add Red Onion and Optional Ingredients:**
    - Scatter thinly sliced red onion over the salad. If using, sprinkle toasted almonds or chopped pistachios and crumbled goat cheese or feta cheese over the salad.
5. **Drizzle with Dressing:**
    - Drizzle the prepared dressing over the salad ingredients.

6. **Toss Gently:**
   - Gently toss the Citrus Avocado Salad together to combine all the ingredients and coat them with the dressing.
7. **Serve:**
   - Serve the Citrus Avocado Salad immediately as a refreshing and nutritious side dish or light meal.

Tips:

- Use a variety of citrus fruits for a colorful and flavorful salad. You can also add segments of tangerines or mandarins.
- Adjust the sweetness and tanginess of the dressing to your taste by varying the amount of honey or lemon juice.
- If preparing ahead, wait to add the avocado until just before serving to prevent browning.

This Citrus Avocado Salad is perfect for summer gatherings or as a bright addition to any meal. Enjoy the combination of creamy avocado, tangy citrus fruits, crunchy nuts, and zesty dressing in every bite!

Kale Caesar Salad

Ingredients:

For the Salad:

- 1 bunch kale (about 6-8 cups), stems removed and leaves chopped into bite-sized pieces
- 1 cup croutons (homemade or store-bought)
- 1/4 cup grated Parmesan cheese

For the Caesar Dressing:

- 1/2 cup mayonnaise
- 1/4 cup grated Parmesan cheese
- 2 tablespoons fresh lemon juice
- 1 tablespoon Dijon mustard
- 1 clove garlic, minced
- 1 anchovy fillet (optional, for traditional Caesar flavor)
- 1/4 teaspoon Worcestershire sauce
- Salt and freshly ground black pepper, to taste
- Water (to thin dressing, if needed)

Instructions:

1. **Prepare the Dressing:**
   - In a blender or food processor, combine mayonnaise, grated Parmesan cheese, fresh lemon juice, Dijon mustard, minced garlic, anchovy fillet (if using), Worcestershire sauce, salt, and pepper. Blend until smooth. If the dressing is too thick, you can add a tablespoon of water at a time until desired consistency is reached. Taste and adjust seasoning as needed.
2. **Massage the Kale:**
   - Place the chopped kale leaves in a large salad bowl. Drizzle with a little olive oil and a pinch of salt. Massage the kale with your hands for a few minutes until it starts to soften and wilt slightly. This helps to tenderize the kale and improve its texture.
3. **Assemble the Salad:**
   - Add the croutons and grated Parmesan cheese to the bowl with the kale.
4. **Add Dressing:**
   - Pour the prepared Caesar dressing over the kale and toss gently to coat all the leaves evenly with the dressing.

5. **Serve:**
    - Serve the Kale Caesar Salad immediately, garnished with additional Parmesan cheese and freshly ground black pepper if desired.

Tips:

- For a vegetarian version, you can omit the anchovy fillet or substitute it with a teaspoon of capers for a similar briny flavor.
- Make homemade croutons by tossing cubed bread with olive oil, salt, and herbs, then baking in the oven until golden and crispy.
- This salad can be served as a side dish or a main course by adding grilled chicken, shrimp, or tofu.

This Kale Caesar Salad is a nutritious and satisfying dish with a balance of flavors and textures, making it a perfect addition to any meal or as a light lunch option. Enjoy the robust flavors of the Caesar dressing combined with the hearty kale leaves!

Roasted Beet and Goat Cheese Salad

Ingredients:

For the Salad:

- 3-4 medium-sized beets, preferably mixed colors (red, golden, or Chioggia), peeled and cut into wedges
- 4 cups mixed salad greens (such as arugula, baby spinach, or mixed greens)
- 1/2 cup crumbled goat cheese
- 1/4 cup toasted walnuts or pecans, chopped
- Optional: 1/4 cup dried cranberries or pomegranate seeds

For the Vinaigrette:

- 1/4 cup extra virgin olive oil
- 2 tablespoons balsamic vinegar
- 1 tablespoon honey or maple syrup
- 1 teaspoon Dijon mustard
- Salt and freshly ground black pepper, to taste

Instructions:

1. Roast the Beets:
   - Preheat the oven to 400°F (200°C). Place the beet wedges on a baking sheet lined with parchment paper. Drizzle with olive oil and season with salt and pepper. Roast for 25-30 minutes, or until the beets are tender when pierced with a fork. Remove from the oven and let them cool slightly.
2. Prepare the Vinaigrette:
   - In a small bowl, whisk together the extra virgin olive oil, balsamic vinegar, honey or maple syrup, Dijon mustard, salt, and pepper until well combined. Adjust seasoning to taste.
3. Assemble the Salad:
   - Arrange the mixed salad greens on a serving platter or in a salad bowl.
4. Add Roasted Beets:
   - Top the greens with the roasted beet wedges.
5. Sprinkle with Goat Cheese and Nuts:
   - Scatter crumbled goat cheese and toasted walnuts or pecans over the salad.
6. Optional: Add Dried Fruit:

- If using, sprinkle dried cranberries or pomegranate seeds over the salad for a touch of sweetness and color.
7. Drizzle with Vinaigrette:
    - Drizzle the prepared vinaigrette over the salad ingredients.
8. Serve:
    - Serve the Roasted Beet and Goat Cheese Salad immediately, garnished with additional cracked black pepper if desired.

Tips:

- For easier preparation, you can roast the beets ahead of time and store them in the refrigerator until ready to use.
- Adjust the sweetness and acidity of the vinaigrette to your taste by varying the amount of honey or balsamic vinegar.
- This salad pairs well with grilled chicken or salmon for a more substantial meal.

Enjoy the vibrant flavors and textures of this Roasted Beet and Goat Cheese Salad as a delicious and nutritious addition to your meal!

Chickpea and Avocado Salad

Ingredients:

For the Salad:

- 1 can (15 ounces) chickpeas (garbanzo beans), drained and rinsed
- 1 large avocado, diced
- 1/2 cucumber, diced
- 1/4 cup red onion, finely chopped
- 1/4 cup cherry tomatoes, halved
- 1/4 cup fresh cilantro or parsley, chopped
- Optional: 1/4 cup crumbled feta cheese or goat cheese
- Optional: 1/4 cup toasted sunflower seeds or chopped almonds

For the Dressing:

- 2 tablespoons extra virgin olive oil
- 1 tablespoon fresh lemon juice
- 1 clove garlic, minced
- 1 teaspoon Dijon mustard
- Salt and freshly ground black pepper, to taste

Instructions:

1. **Prepare the Dressing:**
    - In a small bowl, whisk together the extra virgin olive oil, fresh lemon juice, minced garlic, Dijon mustard, salt, and pepper until well combined. Set aside.
2. **Assemble the Salad:**
    - In a large salad bowl, combine the drained and rinsed chickpeas, diced avocado, diced cucumber, finely chopped red onion, halved cherry tomatoes, and chopped fresh cilantro or parsley.
3. **Add Optional Ingredients:**
    - If using, add crumbled feta cheese or goat cheese and toasted sunflower seeds or chopped almonds to the salad bowl.
4. **Pour Dressing Over Salad:**
    - Drizzle the prepared dressing over the salad ingredients.
5. **Toss Gently:**
    - Gently toss all the ingredients together until the chickpeas, avocado, and vegetables are evenly coated with the dressing.

6. **Serve:**
    - Serve the Chickpea and Avocado Salad immediately as a satisfying and nutritious meal on its own or as a side dish.

Tips:

- For added flavor, you can sprinkle the salad with a pinch of paprika or cumin.
- Adjust the acidity of the dressing by adding more lemon juice if desired.
- This salad can be made ahead of time and stored in the refrigerator. Add the avocado just before serving to prevent browning.

Enjoy this Chickpea and Avocado Salad as a delicious way to incorporate fiber, healthy fats, and fresh vegetables into your diet!

Mexican Corn Salad

Ingredients:

- 4 cups fresh corn kernels (about 4-5 ears of corn)
- 2 tablespoons mayonnaise
- 2 tablespoons sour cream or Mexican crema
- 1/2 cup crumbled cotija cheese or feta cheese
- 1/4 cup finely chopped red onion
- 1/4 cup chopped fresh cilantro
- 1 jalapeño pepper, seeded and finely chopped (optional for heat)
- 1 clove garlic, minced
- 1 tablespoon lime juice (about 1 lime)
- 1/2 teaspoon chili powder (adjust to taste)
- Salt and freshly ground black pepper, to taste
- Lime wedges, for serving

Instructions:

1. **Cook the Corn:**
    - If using fresh corn, shuck the ears and remove silk. Steam or boil the corn until tender, about 5-7 minutes. Alternatively, you can grill the corn for a smoky flavor. Once cooked, let the corn cool slightly, then cut the kernels off the cob.
2. **Prepare the Dressing:**
    - In a large bowl, whisk together the mayonnaise, sour cream or Mexican crema, minced garlic, lime juice, chili powder, salt, and pepper until well combined.
3. **Assemble the Salad:**
    - Add the cooked corn kernels, crumbled cotija cheese or feta cheese, finely chopped red onion, chopped cilantro, and jalapeño (if using) to the bowl with the dressing.
4. **Mix Well:**
    - Gently toss all the ingredients together until the corn kernels are evenly coated with the dressing and other ingredients.
5. **Chill (Optional):**
    - For best flavor, refrigerate the Mexican Corn Salad for at least 30 minutes before serving to allow the flavors to meld together.
6. **Serve:**

- Serve the Mexican Corn Salad chilled or at room temperature. Garnish with additional crumbled cheese, chopped cilantro, and lime wedges on the side.

Tips:

- You can adjust the spiciness by adding more or less jalapeño, or leaving it out entirely if you prefer a milder flavor.
- If cotija cheese is not available, crumbled feta cheese makes a great substitute.
- This salad pairs well with grilled meats, seafood, or as a topping for tacos.

Enjoy the vibrant flavors of this Mexican Corn Salad as a delicious and festive addition to your meal!

Herbed Potato Salad

Ingredients:

- 2 lbs (about 1 kg) potatoes (such as Yukon Gold or red potatoes), peeled or unpeeled, cut into bite-sized cubes
- 1/2 cup mayonnaise
- 1/4 cup plain Greek yogurt or sour cream
- 2 tablespoons Dijon mustard
- 2 tablespoons apple cider vinegar or white wine vinegar
- 1/4 cup chopped fresh herbs (such as parsley, dill, chives, or a combination)
- 1/4 cup finely chopped red onion
- 2 celery stalks, finely chopped
- Salt and freshly ground black pepper, to taste

Instructions:

1. **Cook the Potatoes:**
   - Place the potato cubes in a large pot and cover with cold water. Add a generous pinch of salt. Bring to a boil over medium-high heat, then reduce heat to medium and simmer until potatoes are tender when pierced with a fork, about 10-15 minutes. Drain the potatoes and let them cool slightly.
2. **Prepare the Dressing:**
   - In a large bowl, whisk together the mayonnaise, Greek yogurt or sour cream, Dijon mustard, apple cider vinegar or white wine vinegar, chopped herbs, chopped red onion, and celery. Season with salt and pepper to taste.
3. **Assemble the Salad:**
   - Add the cooked and slightly cooled potatoes to the bowl with the dressing. Gently toss to coat the potatoes evenly with the dressing.
4. **Chill (Optional):**
   - For best flavor, refrigerate the Herbed Potato Salad for at least 1 hour before serving to allow the flavors to meld together.
5. **Serve:**
   - Serve the Herbed Potato Salad chilled or at room temperature. Garnish with additional chopped herbs if desired.

Tips:

- You can adjust the creaminess of the salad by varying the ratio of mayonnaise to Greek yogurt or sour cream.
- Feel free to add other ingredients like diced pickles, capers, or hard-boiled eggs for extra flavor and texture.
- This salad can be made ahead of time and stored in the refrigerator for up to 2-3 days.

Enjoy this Herbed Potato Salad as a delicious and versatile side dish that complements a variety of main courses!

Cranberry Almond Quinoa Salad

Ingredients:

For the Salad:

- 1 cup quinoa, rinsed
- 2 cups water or vegetable broth
- 1/2 cup dried cranberries
- 1/2 cup sliced almonds, toasted
- 1/4 cup chopped fresh parsley or cilantro
- 1/4 cup finely chopped red onion (optional)

For the Dressing:

- 1/4 cup extra virgin olive oil
- 2 tablespoons apple cider vinegar or white wine vinegar
- 1 tablespoon maple syrup or honey
- 1 teaspoon Dijon mustard
- 1 clove garlic, minced
- Salt and freshly ground black pepper, to taste

Instructions:

1. **Cook the Quinoa:**
    - In a medium saucepan, combine the quinoa and water or vegetable broth. Bring to a boil, then reduce heat to low, cover, and simmer for 15-20 minutes, or until quinoa is cooked and liquid is absorbed. Remove from heat and let it cool.
2. **Prepare the Dressing:**
    - In a small bowl, whisk together the extra virgin olive oil, apple cider vinegar or white wine vinegar, maple syrup or honey, Dijon mustard, minced garlic, salt, and pepper until well combined.
3. **Assemble the Salad:**
    - In a large salad bowl, combine the cooked and cooled quinoa with dried cranberries, toasted sliced almonds, chopped fresh parsley or cilantro, and finely chopped red onion (if using).
4. **Add Dressing:**
    - Pour the prepared dressing over the salad ingredients.
5. **Toss Gently:**

- Gently toss all the ingredients together until the quinoa, cranberries, almonds, and herbs are evenly coated with the dressing.
6. **Chill (Optional):**
    - For best flavor, refrigerate the Cranberry Almond Quinoa Salad for at least 30 minutes before serving to allow the flavors to meld together.
7. **Serve:**
    - Serve the Cranberry Almond Quinoa Salad chilled or at room temperature. Garnish with additional chopped herbs or toasted almonds if desired.

Tips:

- To toast almonds, spread them in a single layer on a baking sheet and bake at 350°F (175°C) for 5-7 minutes, stirring halfway through, until lightly golden and fragrant.
- Adjust the sweetness and acidity of the dressing to your taste preference by varying the amount of maple syrup or vinegar.
- This salad can be stored in the refrigerator in an airtight container for up to 3-4 days.

Enjoy this Cranberry Almond Quinoa Salad as a nutritious and satisfying dish on its own or as a side to grilled chicken or fish!

www.ingramcontent.com/pod-product-compliance
Lightning Source LLC
LaVergne TN
LVHW061939070526
838199LV00060B/3883